THINK BIG
SCALE FAST

The Marketing Scaleur's Secrets to Successfully Growing a Business

JOLIEN DEMEYER

MARKETING SCALEURS PUBLISHING
CHICAGO, ILLINOIS

Marketing Scaleurs Publishing
Chicago, IL
www.MarketingScaleurs.com

Ordering Information: Special discounts are available for bulk purchases.
To inquire, please email the publisher or visit our website.

Think Big, Scale Fast
The Marketing Scaleur's Secrets to Successfully Growing a Business

Cover Design: Boja, http://portfolio.jelenamirkovic.com

Interior Design: GKS Creative, https://gkscreative.com/

First Printing, 2020

ISBN Print: 978-1-7356897-0-8
ISBN e-Readers: 978-1-7356897-1-5

Printed in the United States of America

Contents

Preface

In the business world, performance management is driven by Key Performance Indicators (KPIs), those ubiquitous metrics that gauge whether a company, department, team, or individual is meeting its goals — or falling short. KPIs are useful because they compartmentalize performance into discrete, often-quantifiable categories and systematize their evaluation. They make it possible to make sense of the nebulous, dynamic, frequently chaotic "system" of an organization or an employee. KPIs provide clarity about where we are and where we're going.

The language of KPIs is unabashed corporate-speak; you probably wouldn't use them to evaluate a first date (although it's not the worst idea!). But there is a way to apply the same kind of KPI-based evaluation to our own lives.

One of my most significant personal and professional breakthroughs — which partly inspired me to write this book — came when I started thinking about my life in KPI terms, just as I had for so many years in the organizations where I had worked and excelled.

The epiphany came one night when I was on a business trip, consulting with a client about how to expand their operations into new markets. As I was relaxing in the hotel room after a long day of meetings, I had a stroke of inspiration. I set the hotel notepad in front of me and began writing, listing KPIs for my own life — at work, home, and play. These were criteria I would use to measure whether I was on the right track; objectives that, once accomplished, would signal that I was making optimal use of my time, energy, and intellect.

The list was varied, from professional goals (attain a top managerial position by X year; launch my own company by Y year) to intellectual development (read two books a month) to fun "bucket list" experiences (eat sushi in Japan; smoke a cigar in Havana).

Although these "life KPIs" were diverse, a common trait linked everything from skydiving to founding a startup: a great eagerness to constantly be learning, developing, and improving. That's the trait that has kept me going my whole life.

In essence, I realized, the KPIs were secondary to a more important revelation: I was seeking to "scale myself."

The concept of scaling was not new to me. For a long time, I had been helping the firms that employed me do just that. But now I saw it in a more personal, emotionally resonant light. In this book, I've synthesized my "life-scaling" methodology — formulated during a successful career in marketing at some of the world's top firms — into a complete guide for scaleurs: entrepreneurs who wish to scale their businesses, and especially their marketing activities or the marketing departments of their companies.

As a global scaling professional and expert in brands and marketing, I possess a finely honed aptitude for building things, a trait that was evident from an early age, when my strong affinity for Legos provided an outlet for assembling small pieces into perfect, whole forms.

This talent served me well at Lantmännen Unibake, the global frozen bakery company where I began my career before being promoted to senior category manager. That position put me in the driver's seat to launch products for various channels, with the responsibility of making the category profitable. As I started to listen to salespeople, visit customers, and confer with managers in the firm, I discovered what was missing in the business: a way to buy or trade finished goods that we needed to develop our products but could not produce ourselves in our own bakeries. Before I knew it, I was working to create a trading department within Unibake to address this gap and ensure a full-scale portfolio.

I envisioned a trading company that would provide a one-stop shop for customers. By adding new products to our portfolio, we could expand our clientele and then our market share.

Internally, I faced opposition because the prevailing mindset was that this wouldn't be profitable because it meant buying a product from a third party, which marked up their price, and then selling our resulting product through a wholesaler. Moreover, the managers thought that expanding our portfolio would create extra work and raise quality control issues, because we would now have a new line of products to monitor.

There was some merit to these objections, but the main issue was overcoming resistance to change and being open to trying new things (a necessary mindset if you're going to scale your marketing department or business). Ultimately, the trading company was established — and ended up being more profitable than the business as a whole. It was a great example of scaling. The lesson learned was that small efforts, standardized systems, a solid strategy, and the addition of new products could result in serving far more customers — as long as you had the essentials in your product portfolio.

I set my sights on the international market and persuaded the higher-ups to revamp our export department. At the time, we focused on the regional market — our own country of Belgium, plus the Netherlands, France, Italy, and Spain. We expanded to Croatia, Denmark, Norway, Poland, and the United States. After daily flights to talk to lots of customers, and inviting them for product demos, I learned what customer centricity really meant: truly understanding your customer's gains and pain points. In one year, sales — my core responsibility — increased from $36 million to $40 million. As a result, I had the opportunity to move to one of our sister companies in Chicago to be part of the marketing team and scale their business in similar ways. Without hesitation, I packed up and left Belgium, ready to tackle whatever cultural and workplace differences awaited me. In the Chicago office, I focused on reviving a stagnant digital marketing department and evolved into becoming a digital marketing expert.

Even as I thrived in this role, I never lost my passion for "scaling myself." I made amazing friends, established a flourishing network (both personal and professional), and took the opportunity to see a large swath of my adopted new country. On the academic front, I earned a digital analytics certification from MIT. This supplemented my master's in management from the Vlerick International Business School in Belgium, as well as a masters in Economics in Ehsal Belgium, and an EMBA from Hult International Business School in London.

Throughout my career, an insatiable drive for learning new things has contributed to my personal growth mindset, which is an essential ingredient of being a scaleur.

At this point in my career, I made my own move. Encouraged by my mentor, I started my own company, called P-Poka, which means "popcorn" in Portuguese. I chose that name because my brain is like a popcorn popper — tons of ideas pop into my mind, and when my mind fixates on something, I become hungry and curious to figure it out and solve challenges until achieving my goals.

Six months after starting P-Poka, I launched Marketing Scaleurs Inc. in Chicago, as a subsidiary of my Belgium company, P-Poka. After just three months in business, we had a team of four people and six large customers.

In starting Marketing Scaleurs, I was eager to build processes that were scalable, put the right team together, make a strategic roadmap for the company's long-term outlook, and have fun while doing all this. When a job is fun and you get excited about it, you will go the extra mile.

I hope you can learn to find your passion and how to scale your business, too. You don't have to go it alone. I'll share the lessons I've learned so scaling doesn't have to seem like an impossible dream, but a feasible goal any scaleur can achieve.

Introduction

Every entrepreneur wishes for more of two things: time and money. We yearn for more time because balancing any semblance of a career with the demands of a family life, friends, and other interests becomes overwhelming. We desire more money so we can run ads or expand our marketing operations, and do everything else in between that leads to success. Yes, having more time or money would be great, but they are both wasted if you don't know how to spend or properly invest them in marketing or growing your business.

Of all the challenges small-business owners face, scaling their business is one of the hardest. Marketing organizations — whether a department or a single-service company — are under a tremendous amount of pressure to perform, yet budgets aren't growing even while expectations are. How do you do more with less, without compromising on quality? You also want to capitalize on your success, but you fear you won't be able to consistently offer the personal touch that customers rely on, or you'll compromise quality by bringing on additional staff, or you'll dilute your brand if you grow too quickly.

On the other hand, demand for your products and services is steadily growing, and you see even more opportunities — if you could just figure out how to scale.

Scaling a business means setting the stage to support growth in your company. It means having the ability to grow without being hampered. It requires planning; some funding; and the right systems, staff, processes, technology, and partners.

For marketing leaders at growing companies who are ready to expand their programs, scaling marketing is a top priority. But doing so comes with major challenges: Coordinating different teams while managing priorities, resources, and metrics in a way that doesn't slow everyone down is no easy task. Bigger doesn't have to mean slower or less effective, though. By scaling your marketing, your growing organization can stay lean and agile while continuing to deliver campaigns that impress customers and fuel business growth.

While there are a lot of books and blogs about the challenges of scaling a small business, we'll focus on scaling your marketing. This will put you in a position to scale your business, saving more time *and* more money.

Congratulations — you've made the decision to grow your business! Get ready for the next challenge: how to scale your business for growth.

PART ONE

Are You Ready to Become a Scaleur?

Before moving on, I want to ask you an extremely important question, one that very few business owners ever ask themselves: If you were hit by a bus tomorrow (or otherwise incapacitated), what would happen to your business?

The unfortunate reality is that most business owners build a job for themselves, not a business. Their companies depend on them showing up to run them, day in and day out, and most founders lack a defined exit strategy. In fact, many successful entrepreneurs are so busy with daily operations that they don't have the time or energy left to grow and develop the business. If they aren't present each day, their businesses suffer — in many cases grinding to a halt.

Entrepreneurs launch their own businesses to have freedom, but are you really free if you don't control your time and what you do with it, even though you own the company? Isn't that one of the foremost reasons you became an entrepreneur: to control your own schedule and enjoy the time and freedom to do what you want, when you want?

To scale your marketing efforts, you will need to build a *business*, not a job.

Scaling vs. Growth

After the technology boom of the past decade, the most successful companies have shown that the path to success isn't all about growth — it's about scaling. They've learned how to create business models that easily scale to generate massive revenues without adding massive costs and resources along the way.

Many entrepreneurs are often confused by the difference between growth and scaling. Growing means a department or entire business adds new resources (capital, people, or technology), and its revenue increases as a result. For instance, a marketing department may gain $50,000 in new revenue, but to do so, they have to hire a new marketing person with a $50,000 salary. The company's gains and losses are equalized, so although the company is growing — by one new employee and a corresponding uptick in revenue — it really hasn't gained much value. At least, not at first.

Scaling, on the other hand, is when revenue increases without a substantial increase in expenditures. Processes can be "scaled" in a cost-effective manner. Scaling is the process of growing exponentially. A marketing department that spends $5,000 on automation tools to allow more-efficient marketing to a wider audience — gaining $50,000 in new revenue as a result — is scaling. The company's gains outpace its losses, allowing it not only to grow but also to scale.

Other examples include being able to go from handling five clients to 500 or sending out emails to 10 people vs. 1 million — without a major increase in cost or labor. Figure P1.1, "Scaling vs. Growing," illustrates such an expansion.

Figure P1.1: Scaling vs. Growing

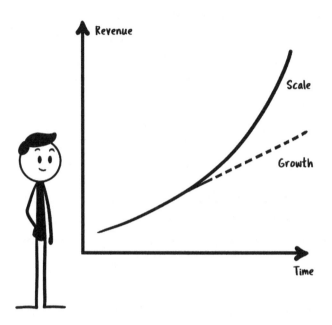

Marketing for your business scales when it can cope with an increase in work while maintaining or increasing its efficiency.

When it comes to scaling your marketing, there are some great factors in success.

- **Automated processes:** Do you have a standard outbound and/or sales process and system in place? When you reach out to new customers, do you have a playbook that describes what you need to say on your first call vs. your third call? The same goes for LinkedIn messages or emails, responses to your website, and related activities. The message is clear: Make a playbook to optimize your process, in part so you don't have to reinvent the wheel at every growth point. The playbook tells everyone what to say and what to do.

- **Subscription-based services:** Do you have systems in place so every year, you start with money in the pipeline? One example is when customers can pay for your service/tool with an annual or monthly subscription.

- **Diverse income streams:** Don't bet on only one income stream. You can get money from a product you offer, a service/consultancy, or training/an academy, etc.

- **High customer retention rates:** For most businesses, 20% of your customers produce 80% of your sales. Repeat customers spend more, generate larger transactions, and bring in additional business by word of mouth.

- **A value ladder of products:** This allows you to cater to your customers' needs (e.g., at the very bottom of the value ladder, create free content in exchange for customers' email addresses). As clients ascend the ladder, the value level increases, as does the cost to play (e.g., give away a downloadable PDF about the five biggest mistakes scaleurs make when scaling their marketing team, then offer an ebook, such as *How to Reach the Scaleur Mindset*, for $19). Farther up the ladder, you can market an online training course, like "How to Scale from 1 Lead to 1 Billion," for $99. From there, you can pitch a one-year program for $999, ultimately ending with coaching for $2,500 per year.

- **Dedicated KPIs you can track on a dashboard:** This is your visual success panel for the company. Focus on key indicators, instead of tackling everything at once.

Companies scale their marketing activity when their revenue increases and their marketing and operating costs remain static. If a company increases their revenue but increases their costs at the same rate, then that business is not scaling.

To find scalable aspects in your marketing model, you must locate the aspects of your marketing business that can be replicated quickly and cost-effectively, while still building a strong marketing organization.

When Is the Right Time to Scale Your Business?

There is no magic formula for identifying exactly the right time to scale your business. However, there are many things you should have figured out before you decide to take that step.

Scaling is all about using rapid-growth strategies to add new customers and grow your revenue. Scaling a business or its marketing department mainly depends on two factors: capability and capacity. Ask yourself:

- Is your business capable enough to grow?

- Does it have the capacity to accommodate growth?

In the context of business, scalability describes the ability of the business to grow without being hampered by limited resources when production increases.

Technology is an important component of the equation. You need to assess your current technological capacity and technological needs in the future as you scale.

Technology has facilitated scalability in recent years by making it much easier to acquire customers and expand markets, opening unprecedented opportunities for businesses to go global. The latest user-friendly apps and tech tools have changed how people think about interacting with or purchasing from a business. Today, you can link to and purchase from businesses all over the world, just by viewing a website or an Instagram ad. With any web search, ads trigger you to buy the things you are searching for.

Entrepreneurs work long hours and dedicate their lives to their ventures. When success finally comes, it is certainly cause for celebration, but it also brings new challenges. After all, if the marketing business starts to scale without truly understanding who the customer is or whether the demand is sustainable, growth can derail quickly.

Other main indications that will help you figure out when it's time to take that next step and scale include:

- Employees are unable to handle the workload.

- Long-term marketing goals are unachievable.

- Leads continue to increase.

- Your numbers say you're good to go — specifically, your income shows steady growth rather than extreme fluctuations or no growth at all.

- You have a steadily growing income stream rather than one that jumps up and down every month.

In addition, ask yourself these questions:

- **Do you have a plan to move forward?** An-of-year goal? What are the main KPIs you will use to determine that the year was successful? What does success look like two years from now?

- **Do you have marketing processes in place, and are they the right ones?** Marketing processes take many different forms. Depending on where a lead is in the sales funnel, identify ways to market a service (we'll discuss sales funnels in more depth in the "9 Key Marketing Metrics" section in Rule 4.). Nurture potential customers by providing a free service, for instance. It is essential that no matter how you plan to scale your business, you have documented systems in place to accommodate your marketing's structure. Does your sales team know what to do when a lead comes in? Explain where the lead comes from and what you expect from them. Create and work with a playbook. (In the next section, we will talk more about putting scalable processes in place.)

- **Do you have the right technology in place?** Both technology and connectivity play key roles in the growth of your marketing activities. You'll need a clear vision of what your business needs before scaling it forward, both in terms of functionality and cost. Know where you want to go in the long term — you might need to buy a tool despite its significant initial cost, rather than lease or subscribe to it and continue paying for it again and again, if it's a great resource that will save money in the long term.

- **Do you have the right team in place?** Rarely can businesses scale without hiring talent in some capacity. You will probably have to let go of some employees while hiring new people to support your goals as you grow the business. Your team must be open to doing new things and experimenting. Scaling your marketing is an ongoing change process.

- **Do you have enough demand?** Just because your business may be booming now doesn't mean it will be sustainable indefinitely. One of the biggest challenges marketers faces when scaling is being able to attract enough customers and clients to support their growth. Before you scale, you have to understand your market trends and forecasts by undertaking a rigorous analysis. Don't base your direction only on emotions or assumptions — make sure the new leads are qualified and worth following. If inbound leads are high, you can start scaling, but you must understand the foundations.

- **Are your finances in order?** Uncertainty comes with change. Having a financial plan to accommodate the immediate "what ifs" that may occur mitigates the unknown. Put together some projections to see whether your marketing budget can pay for business essentials as you progress. For example, when I first started working with the company CHD Expert, a global foodservice database provider, I made a blueprint outlining what they had and a roadmap of what I wanted to achieve in the first year. I asked myself what would make me happy by the end of the year. Similarly, you can make a list of "must haves" vs. "nice to haves" for your business. Your budget must be based on the must-haves, but can include some nice-to-haves for experimentation.

- **Do you know your customers' expectations?**
  When considering expansion, it is imperative to
  keep your customers and their expectations at the
  forefront. Your marketing tactics should revolve
  around their wants and needs — not yours. Spend
  less time worrying about day-to-day logistics and
  more time on connecting and innovating with your
  customers. Involve your customers in what you are
  doing: Ask them questions, make a dedicated survey
  for them to fill out, and reward them for their loyalty
  and feedback. It sounds simple, but go with the basics.
  For example, I work with A-SAFE, a world-leading
  safety barrier innovator. When I began working with
  them, I started by doing a survey that consisted of 15
  questions for each of its current 1,500 leads. It wasn't
  a big ask, but response was low. The problem was the
  reward for the customer was not mentioned in the
  subject line. Why would a customer waste their time?

By scrutinizing all these aspects of your business and
answering these questions candidly, you'll be ready to scale
your business successfully and set yourself up for the growth
you've been looking for. At the same time, you'll highlight weak
areas to develop before undertaking your mission of scaling the
business and its marketing activities for greater success. If you
set a vision of developing a scalable business, you start with
creating a blueprint and then move into automating processes.

Scaling your business means building on a foundation that
can serve more customers with the same resources. It isn't
something you do once. It's something you'll do regularly
throughout the life of your business.

You've learned the "why" you should scale your business in Part 1. In Part 2, we'll talk about accomplishing the "how" by following four fundamental rules — the 4 S's — for putting a scaling vision into practice.

PART TWO

The 4 S's for Scaling Your Marketing and Business

Roughly 50 million startups are born each year[1] with the intention of eventually becoming profitable businesses. Entrepreneurs dream of beginning their startups with next to nothing in the bank and growing their businesses into million-dollar companies. But the truth is, you may not be ready to scale your business this way.

If growth causes your company to stumble because of confusion, orders falling through the cracks, insufficient staff, miscommunication, inadequate manufacturing, or insufficient delivery capacity, you'll have unhappy customers. Manual processes that worked fine when you were small now won't let you move fast enough. You'll either be putting out fires or desperately trying to keep your head above water. The stress will begin to mount, and you will start to panic at the thought of seeing your entrepreneurial vision go up in smoke — just when you thought you were on the cusp of taking things to the next level.

---

1   http://www.moyak.com/papers/business-startups-entrepreneurs.html.

The research firm Startup Genome surveyed more than 3,200 startups and found that 74% of them fail due to premature scaling.[2] If you don't start out with the right business model or the right systems in place, then it is almost impossible to scale effectively.

Start with a Marketing Plan

To make sure you have the right systems in place, one of your first jobs is to write a marketing plan. You might feel overwhelmed, but do not worry: You can take most of the marketing plans and ideas described in the next chapter and scale them to your specific business needs, audience, and strategies.

To create a traditional marketing plan for your product or service, every marketer knows you must answer the 4 P's:

1. What's your product/service?

2. What's your price?

3. What's your promotion?

4. What's the place?

Once you have addressed these four questions and you have a good market fit, you can start thinking about the 4 Scaling S's, which will be instrumental in putting your plan into action.

What are the 4 S's? This section outlines the 4 S's, which will be crucial for scaling your business:

- **Rule 1:** The Desire to Scale: The Scaleur's Mindset — Have a *scaleur's mindset* and *scaleur team*.

---

2 http://gallery.mailchimp.com/8c534f3b5ad611c0ff8aeccd5/files/ Startup_Genome_Report_Extra_Premature_Scaling_version_2.1.pdf.

- **Rule 2:** Ensuring Your Strategy Is Scalable — Create a scalable *strategy* for where you want to be.

- **Rule 3:** Establishing Standardized Systems — Have scalable *systems* and processes to automate and scale up.

- **Rule 4:** What Can't Be Measured Can't Be Improved: Success Panel — Have a *success panel* to track your performance.

Now that we've introduced the four fundamental rules — the 4 S's — we can delve into putting our scaling vision into practice. In the next chapter, we'll start with Rule 1 and learn about the scaleur's mindset.

RuLe 1

Entrepreneurs Must Have the Desire to Scale: The Scaleur's Mindset

Just as it takes a certain entrepreneurial way of thinking to embark on the challenge of founding a business, scalability is a mindset, too. You need to think big to become big. Having a scalable business means that you are free to unleash your dreams, make a lot of money, and have fun doing it. Once you get your mind in the game, scalability becomes much easier.

Being a *scaleur* means being an entrepreneur who also has the perspicacity, confidence, and dedication to scale their business.

In the early stages of an incipient business, most owners are focused on growth — growing their lead base, increasing revenue, and bringing on more employees to perform various functions.

Growth in marketing can take you from one lead to 100, but to get from 100 to 100,000, you'll have to scale. Growth depends on individual decisions made in the moment, but scaling is built on predictable, repeatable processes designed with efficiency in mind. If you have strong processes, you can hire new employees, provide instructions for how to perform a task, and get consistent results within days instead of months.

Scaleurs think differently about their businesses: They don't merely want to expand by working proportionally harder. Instead, they look for smart processes that allow for a huge bump in productivity and profit with a comparatively smaller uptick in labor and resource expenditures. We can divide entrepreneurs into two groups: ones with a fixed mindset vs. those with a growth mindset, or scaleurs (see Figure 1.1: Fixed vs. Growth Mindset).

Fixed Mindset

It's been said that "believing that your qualities are carved in stone — the fixed mindset — creates an urgency to prove yourself over and over. If you only have a certain amount of intelligence, a certain personality, and a certain moral character ... well, then, you'd better prove that you have a healthy dose of them. It simply wouldn't do to look deficient in these most basic characteristics."[3]

This group has a defined identity and often uses labels and affirmations. They see situations and qualities as unchangeable and their skills and capabilities as fixed. The strengths and behaviors that allowed them to successfully navigate the early stages of their businesses won't be sufficient for scaling or could even work against them in the process.

During my career, I have met a lot of people with this mindset. When moving from Europe to America, I was seen as not only the new person at the company but also a "European spy." People didn't trust me, and consequently, they did not trust the work I was doing. Here a few examples of things I would often hear, and my responses:

---

3 https://medium.com/leadership-motivation-and-impact/fixed-v-growth-mindset-902e7d0081b3.

- "I already know all I need to know; you cannot teach me more."

  My response: Einstein never stopped learning about physics, did he?

- "What's the point in trying to understand the CRM [customer relationship management] if I'm going to fail anyway?"

  My response: Is failing not a learning experience unto itself? Failing doesn't mean you can't do something; it just means you haven't gotten it right yet.

- "Yet another guest speaker or external consultant. What is she going to bring, except cost?"

  My response: Use this opportunity to learn something new and expand your skills repertoire; make yourself adaptable, relevant, and even more useful. You never know where your abilities might take you.

- "I am intimidated by the success of others."

  My response: It is common to be jealous of or intimidated by others' success, but more often than not, they are normal people like yourself.

- "You had the chance to earn a master's. You got the promotion. You had the chance to go abroad. I won't be as lucky."

  My response: It's your life, and you are free to choose your path and your destinations. Walk your own path and get advice from the people you admire. You are stronger with two.

- "I know my customers and clients. Leave me alone. I have my own routine that works for me."

  My response: Let's leave the hard no-ers alone and work with those whom we can influence. After a while, the holdouts should see the results and open up to the new approach. If not, try to let them go — if they don't bring energy and value, fire them, or at least move them to other areas where they won't block progress.

Because of this fixed mindset, it took a lot of time and effort to change the perception of my colleagues in a way that moved the organization forward and spurred creativity and productivity. I identified the people who were able to change and could have an impact, and started to work with them. Walking the walk, showing results, and giving it time were the best strategies to move forward — and getting the people with a fixed mindset to buy in.

Getting that buy-in is not an easy task, and it won't happen overnight. Get management to buy in first. Tell them why it's worth doing, and what's in it for them and their company. Consider learning about Simon Sinek's circle of control. You can start with small steps, like email marketing, which lead to getting feedback from customers. Then you go on the road with the sales team to understand the customers and the sales representatives' opinions about changing the marketing structure. Make a dashboard that tracks activities, so they see the results. You may have to start small and think big.

As much as fixed-mindset thinkers would have you believe that people are born with an innate ability for certain skills and can't grow beyond them, you can build your own skills and abilities extensively. You have to dedicate yourself to the process. Then you can demonstrate your success to the naysayers and encourage them to make similar efforts.

Figure 1.1: Fixed vs. Growth Mindset — Growth Mindset Scaleurs

In the growth mindset, you possess an inborn set of talents, abilities, and interests, and you have the capacity to cultivate and expand them. You believe that everyone is capable of changing, growing, and learning through sustained effort.

This group is constantly evolving. They never view themselves or their businesses as static, finished, complete. Instead, they're constantly on the lookout for ways to serve a larger market, as well as innovating and adding to their products or services. Entrepreneurs with a growth mindset seek ways to add to their skillsets by not being afraid of confronting a challenging situation.

This group welcomes data and feedback, negative or positive, and understands that such input only reinforces their intellectual and professional curiosity. That way of thinking enables continuous innovation and improvement. Change delivers more chances to evolve. Growth-mindset entrepreneurs see the bigger picture of the journey, are more resilient, and have a better chance for long-term success. Here are a few ways to emulate this mindset.

1. **Give up control and delegate.** It's understandable to maintain a tight grip on everything in the beginning stages. You do most of the work, along with your co-founder and maybe another team member. Processes are not documented, so you're used to overseeing everything closely. But when it's time to scale, you have to find a way to delegate appropriately — not leaving the scene, but learning to trust and build your people up: giving them the right tools to execute without you and helping them realize their potential, too. Don't micromanage. For example, my mentor, Lionel, was only interested in results. If the results were good, he was fine with however you worked to achieve them. But if the weekly and monthly results started to slack, he would reexamine the methodology to find out how we could improve the system. Having a dashboard to follow your KPIs is immensely helpful for this aspect of scaling.

2. Embrace challenges as growth experiences. The easiest way to do this is to simply ask yourself in the face of difficulty (or in the face of success, too): "What might be the opportunity here?" This will help you approach a given situation from a more open, optimistic perspective and offer different angles on how to solve the problem.

I often encourage entrepreneurs to ask themselves this simple question: "What's the worst that can happen?" Often, we subconsciously exaggerate the gravity or risk of a challenge just because it's new or unfamiliar. When you think through what might occur, you often discover that the worst possible outcome is, in fact, not that bad.

3. See the bigger picture by breaking up the path to reach it into tactical steps. It is now time to build necessary systems and, most important, to work on your strategy. As much as the creative side and the experimental phases are fun, scaling needs more structure. Instead of immediate gains, seek ways to implement tactical steps to follow a long-term strategy. Setting these in place will allow you to free up more time so you can get involved in solving the harder problems.

One of the tactics I like from the CEO of CHD, Lionel, is that every day, you can only focus on five main "buckets." Every morning, write down a list of the things you want to accomplish that day. You'll probably end up with 20 or more things you want to do. Focus on the top five things you want to accomplish (both professional and private) and block off time in your calendar to accomplish them. This will help you focus on the things that matter to you the most: the bigger picture. I'll talk about finding your motivation points in more detail in the Gingerbread Tool.

4. Take ownership. Take ownership of your attitude and leave your ego behind. Having a growth mindset is about being open to admit you can and will fail. Failing is a part of the learning process; the more you get used to sitting with these experiences and growing from them, the more you begin to take ownership and develop a growth mindset..

Adopt a perspective of being in a constant state of becoming and evolving. Everything that happens serves as a test to teach you what works and what doesn't. You must be versatile and embrace change as inevitable and beneficial. You don't have to be the best at everything, but curiosity and being open to learning new things will help you connect the dots and see the big picture. It is important to understand how things fit together so that you see the opportunities for connections inside and outside your company.

In my time in a previous job, trust was in short supply among my colleagues. Trust encourages employees to take ownership — you don't want to let your team down. Instead, we had the culture of every man for himself: "I can count on myself to get the job done. It's the job of the boss or the team as a whole to change such behavior." Since the leadership team in Belgium was divided and self-interested, they often chose to do the right thing for themselves over the right thing for the company. People and departments worked in silos, and each had its own goal. People initiated many projects or initiatives on their own, because they couldn't always rely on others. There was little unified effort or communication among workers and departments.

5. Celebrate the success of others. Noticing and validating the success of other people, and validating partnerships and collaborations, will shift your mindset to a more positive and abundant perspective. There is enough pie to go around for everyone. Once you understand this and practice it, you can enhance your collaborative relationship with your team while maintaining your ability to pursue your own goals.

My client CHD is a leading data player in the foodservice industry. They sell operator data so companies that supply to restaurants can target the most-qualified leads and get their foot in the door first. I joined CHD in January 2020 as the global scale marketer. A great thing we are doing now at CHD is that each week, each department briefly shares recent successes. Together, we look at the dashboard to see if we completed each department's dedicated KPI — for example, increasing the number of demos scheduled, getting new leads via an email campaign, setting up paid media, or starting with pay per click (PPC). These three-minute updates are always followed with a round of encouraging applause.

At the end of the day, you need to think big to achieve big results. Scalability has a lot to do with your mindset, and building from that place makes a difference.

Scale Yourself First: The Gingerbread Tool

Many chief marketing officers embrace the idea of scaling their business but overlook something equally important: Scale yourself first to strengthen your growth mindset.

If you're an ambitious person, you'll inevitably hit a wall. That seems pessimistic, but it's actually a sign you're doing something right. At points throughout your career, you're guaranteed to feel overwhelmed, burned out, uncertain, or defeated. You're probably the kind of person who takes on as much as you can in any given role, so it's not surprising people keep giving you new things to do, new problems to solve. Whether you get to move up, however, depends on what you do next. It's time to scale yourself.

The key to scaling yourself is to understand yourself first. Not just your skills, but also your energy! Energy management is the hidden key to getting more done. It is the management of the combination of physical, emotional (how you feel at a given moment), and mental energy. What drives you, how you recharge, what your ambitions are, what you take from your past, what is going on in your brain, and so on. Get a grip on who you are and what you want to achieve in life to understand where your energy is coming from.

I learned about the Gingerbread Tool (see Figure 1.2: Gingerbread Tool) while working on my master's in management at Vlerick. It will help you find your seven main attention points in life.

Completing this exercise is easy. You simply answer the seven questions in Figure 1.2 and draw the first thing that pops into your head. Here are some other rules:

- Only drawing is allowed (no words can be written).

- Set your alarm for five minutes (when you only have five minutes to accomplish something, you can't overthink).

- Draw the first thing that comes to your mind.

- Don't forget to have fun.

Figure 1.2: Gingerbread Tool

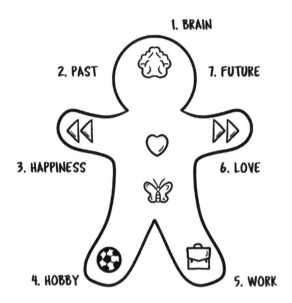

1. Brain: What's the one thing that keeps popping into your head? Examples: Work, family, getting that promotion

2. Past: What's the one thing you take with you from the past? Examples: Prize or award, recognition, a memory of a loved one

3. Happiness: What's the main thing that puts a smile on your face? Examples: Being surrounded by people, having a drink, working, looking after my kids

4. *Hobby:* What do you do for fun? Examples: Hike and camp, go out with friends, attend music concerts

5. *Future:* Where do you see yourself when retired? Examples: A second home, living abroad, being a teacher, involved with a charity

6. *Love:* What's the main thing you love the most? Examples: Your family, being happy, progress

7. *Work:* What's the main thing you want to achieve? Examples: Working 9 to 5, a new promotion, being an entrepreneur, becoming a scaleur

This test is extremely helpful for learning about yourself while aiming to scale as a leader. Understanding your seven main attention points will help you find greater motivation where you're already primed to look for it. It will also help you understand those around you. It will allow you to be extremely effective and persuasive in conversations with others by knowing which way they're oriented.

If done right, this will have a positive impact on your entire company and marketing efforts. Running a business is really not just about you. When you're running a business, it's easy to forget how many people are counting on you to do your job well and on time. There's no greater frustration for a motivated team than to be blocked by their leader. If you scale yourself first, you will get more done than you thought was possible. Then it's time to scale your business itself.

Make Sure Your Team Is Ready

In the beginning, resources will most likely be limited, so it is important to employ the right people with the necessary skillsets to make scaling successful.

Start by looking at your current workload and responsibilities. Are your personnel equipped to handle a ramp-up in projects without neglecting current customers, products, and services? If your marketing coordinators are also supporting other departments (such as PR and customer service) while analyzing performance data and implementing new marketing tools, they're doing too much. Go back and streamline efforts and processes so your team has the bandwidth to scale — or consider adding staff to balance your team's workload and responsibilities.

Next, ask yourself: Does your team have the expertise needed to launch successful campaigns in the new regions or industries you're targeting? If not, should you hire new staff now, or contract out until you have a better idea of the kind of expertise your team needs? Evaluate your current team to identify each member's strengths and expertise, identify where your talent gaps lie, and hire for those roles.

If you need to hire, employ generalists. Marketing is a broad, multifaceted area, and you might need someone who can do PPC, search engine optimization (SEO), and content at the same time. Instead of hiring three people, each with expertise in each field, you can hire a jack-of-all-trades. While this may seem like a loss in quality, it's going to help you long term. A generalist can set up the framework for company operations and lead the rest of the team when you end up hiring for individual roles. Outsource remaining specialized tasks to a third-party organization or freelancers.

Invest in Your A-Team

Some companies, notably big tech companies like Google or Zappos, invest a great deal of money in their employees for good reason: It helps them grow by retaining and attracting top talent. When employees feel valued, they'll passionately share your vision and dig deep within themselves to help your business thrive. Surround yourself with the best people you can and give them an opportunity to do what they love to do best. When people are financially invested, they're looking for a return on that investment. When your employees feel valued, they become emotionally invested and they want to contribute.

Investment also goes beyond perks and benefits. Meet with key people throughout your company. Talk to employees and find out what resources they need to work better and more efficiently. Invest in the resources that will help them today, and scale with operations as your business grows.

Train new hires rigorously. Your first new marketing rep should go through the same training process as your fifth or tenth hire. You can of course tweak your approach to onboarding over time, but your new hires should all have the same opportunities to settle into your marketing process. Rushing or cutting corners in your training will only hurt their performance.

That happens at many companies: They can be like a revolving door. People come and go. There are new hires every month whom nobody knows about. Not fun for the newbies, who just sit at their desks wondering what they are doing, and not fun for the team, who start to think, "Well, here's another one — how long will they last?" New employees are expected to function as if they have already been on the job for five months.

They receive hardly any training, and what little training they do receive is rushed, because the trainers themselves are overworked.

Managers make no effort to explore the strategic reasons *why* additional people were needed.

There is a lack of communication. A new hire appears on the team without the team having been briefed about their arrival. Some are afraid the new person might take their position. Others don't want to invest effort into meeting the new hire.

Some people could be hired to fulfill a role without regard for whether they would fit into the company culture. A candidate who has the right credentials and glowing references can fly through the interview process, only to turn out to be an unexpected problem after hiring.

To head off these problems, take the time to hire the right people and communicate with your team about new people, roles, and objectives. Share the why. Communicate when a vacancy is open. Then, your team members feel acknowledged, they know someone is coming, and they can apply for the new position or promotion if they like. By sharing the objective, you let your team members know what the new person will do, what their responsibility will be, and how it's linked with theirs or their colleagues'.

Finding the Right Scaleurs — A Sample Interview for Your Scaleur A-Team

When recruiting your A-team, it's important that each candidate have the right fit for your company. You want to find people who are hungry, eager to learn and adapt, and have the positive energy to go the extra mile. Having a solid résumé is fine, but you really need them to have a growth mindset.

Here are five questions I like to ask:

1. **What do you want to achieve in life? Where do you want to stand in five or 10 years? When you retire?** This lets you see how ambitious they are.

2. **How would you measure your success?** This shows you how they value their achievements and failures.

3. **On a scale from 0 to 10, how happy are you, and what would it have been last year?** I like to be surrounded with optimistic, positive people. It's OK to feel dissatisfied, but you don't want to waste your energy on hiring someone who complains too much. Everyone gets stuck in traffic jams, but not everyone honks the horn.

4. **What is the most spontaneous thing you did in the last three years?** I want to understand how people feel about going outside their comfort zones.

5. **What makes you happy?** Here, I want to understand their energy drivers.

Overall, these questions relate to me as a person, and help me find out if they are the kind of energizers I want around me. People derive motivation from one another. That is what I am searching for. Everyone has to make their own questions for the hiring process; the Gingerbread Tool will help you understand who you are and which kind of people you need to lift you up — and help your business scale for growth and innovation.

Outsource Strategically

One way of assembling your A-team might involve hiring a marketing consultant, which could save you lots of time and money. Since these professionals have mastered the skill of engaging audiences, they can help you scale your marketing efforts quickly.

Outside consultants may have the staff and investment in systems that enable them to be much more efficient in handling a particular function than your company. Trying to replicate that function internally may take too much time or money. Instead, find a reliable partner to outsource this aspect to, which should position your business to scale better, faster, and cheaper.

However, don't go overboard — "too much of a good thing" can be counterproductive. At a certain moment at one of my previous jobs, we started to feel like the company had more external people than full-time employees. Lots of projects were running with consultants, and many of us felt that management saw them as better than our own people, which was a blow to morale and inhibited collaboration. You have to find the right balance between in-house vs. outsourcing. When you outsource, it is never a bad idea to tell the team why you need the outside help and for how long.

The Relationship Between New Hires and Customer Acquisition Cost

As your business hires experts to improve and streamline processes so the core team can work on scaling the business while sustaining quality, you must ensure that customer satisfaction is not at risk. Moreover, you will need to look at your customer acquisition cost (CAC) (see Figure 1.3: Customer Acquisition Costs).

Once you've reached around $1 million in annual recurring revenue (ARR) and want to accelerate your growth, you need to think about how to scale your marketing team. Many companies are scared to do this, because adding the salaries of new marketers to your budget can cause your CAC to skyrocket.

The strength of the marketing team in a growing company is invaluable—every marketing strategy shapes the way customers will perceive and eventually interact with your product. But the salaries of team members who *work to acquire customers* are a huge factor in your CAC, which is why new marketing hires can be a hit to your CAC metrics. You need to reconcile the cost of scaling to make this investment in your company's future.

CAC is the total cost of sales and marketing efforts needed to acquire a customer. It is one of the defining factors in whether your company has a viable business model that can yield profits by keeping acquisition costs low as you scale.

Figure 1.3: Customer Acquisition Costs

EQUATION:
$$CAC = \frac{\text{Total Cost of Sales \& Marketing}}{\text{\# Of Customers Acquired}}$$

EQUATION:
$$CAC = \left(\frac{\frac{S\&M}{\text{Salaries-Tools-Spend}_1} + \frac{S\&M}{\text{Salaries-Tools-Spend}_2} \cdots \frac{S\&M}{\text{Salaries-Tools-Spend}_n}}{\text{Acquired Customer}_1 + \text{Acquired Customer}_2 \cdots \text{Acquired Customer}_n} \right)$$

EQUATION:
$$CAC = \left(\frac{\$50{,}000 \text{ (Sales \& Marketing Spend)}}{1{,}000 \text{ (Customers Acquired)}} = \$50 \right)$$

Managing these costs is all about maintaining balance, optimizing efficiency, and scaling up customer lifetime value so you can get the maximum return on this investment in your company. You can't make smart business decisions if you don't know the full unit cost for each customer.

Calculating CAC is theoretically straightforward: Divide the total expenses to acquire customers in a certain time period by the number of customers acquired during that period.

But the miscalculations — and the fatal underestimations — of CAC happen when you don't account for all expenses involved with acquiring customers. As you scale, the salaries of your marketing team members become prominent components of your CAC that *you cannot forget to include*. If you don't account for team members in your CAC, you won't really know how much it costs to acquire each customer and you won't be able to determine how to earn back those expenses.

For example, if you assume conservatively that you'll spend $50,000 on an individual marketing team member's annual salary, that's an additional $4,166/month in total expenses to cover by acquiring customers (not including benefits and other possible costs).

Hypothetically, your other costs might total $11,000/month ($1,000 in paid advertising + $10,000 in marketing tools and software). Adding $4,166/month increases monthly CAC by over 37%. Adding two new marketers at that salary means an increase of **over 75%** in your monthly CAC, given these other monthly expenses.

Simply put, the ideal CAC formula is as follows:

CAC = (total cost of sales and marketing)/(# of customers acquired)

For example, if you spend $36,000 to acquire 1,000 customers, your CAC is $36.

CAC = ($36,000 spent)/(1,000 customers) = $36 per customer

This increase shouldn't prevent you from scaling, because with a larger team, you have more power to generate revenue. If your new hires own some of these processes and metrics, you can leverage the power of their addition to improve the quality of your marketing and, ultimately, increase your revenue.

9 Positions in a Winning Marketing Team

Taking your business to the next level means making tough choices and asking yourself what functions you can or should perform — or not perform — internally?

A small company (fewer than 50 employees) may find it unrealistic to have nine different people fill their marketing team positions. Being nimble is a strength for a small business, but it's worth mentioning that lack of structure is an impediment to success. A small company's team structure might consist of fewer players, and in some cases, only one person. Whichever way the company integrates its team, though, the essentials for success remain the same. The following nine positions need not all be separate individuals. It's okay to have an overlap of duties, as long as the structure is sound. Just consider that certain skillsets (and personality types) are more compatible with certain positions than others.

1. **Marketing Manager:** The manager is effectively the coach of the team. This is an essential role that (depending on the size of your team and expertise) an owner could take on or that you can hire for. This person is responsible for managing budgets and communicating the value of the marketing team's efforts to management.

   Some core tasks:

   • Managing/overseeing team performance.

   • Setting and tracking weekly marketing quotas and KPIs based on team performance.

   • Communicating the success of the marketing team to management.

   • Empowering any external marketing partners or agencies by building relationships with them.

   • Managing the budget.

2. **Website Designer/Webmaster:** An entrepreneurial business doesn't necessarily need someone with the traditional "webmaster" title but rather someone who is a master of website design and/or development.

Whenever possible, I'm a believer in managing your website in-house as much as possible, instead of outsourcing to an agency. Because your website is the primary face of your company, it's just too important to put this role in the hands of outsiders. Having your own website designer/webmaster also means having control over timing — not having to wait in line for an agency to get around to your updates, news, and revisions.

If you can find someone who is a hybrid of a designer and a developer, you've struck gold. Otherwise, figure out which side of the coin you value more and target the best talent you can find in that area. Nearly all of your potential customers will visit your website — most begin their journey at that point. Your company's website should be an absolute priority investment, so make sure a skilled person to create and manage it is one of your first hires.

An exceptional developer is the secret weapon for marketing success. The quality of your website's digital experience has a direct impact on your bottom line. Ideally, with a quality developer, you can go from ideation to execution on any digital campaign in months, not years — sometimes even weeks or days.

True conversion rate optimization from your website goes beyond simply changing button colors and instead involves analyzing the entire layout of pages and the user onboarding process. Some tools that can help inform decisions and empower website designers include Hotjar, Optimizely, Google Optimize, and Unbounce. (See Part 3 for a comprehensive list of tools.)

Website-related tasks that affect your bottom line include:

- Designing radical split tests for landing pages. (In a split test, you test different landing pages to see which one gets better traffic.)
- Creating interactive content.
- Fixing site speed issues and finding bugs that hurt conversion rates.
- Adding quality creative material (content, images) to blog posts.
- Reviewing user experiences and improving functionality.
- Rethinking form processes and improving with better design or creative.

Never underestimate the power of good design. Many businesses gloss over this fact and end up with do-it-yourself Photoshop disasters.

3. **SEO Specialist:** Let's face it: Google is still king when it comes to potential customers searching for the products your business offers, and no matter what business you're in, SEO is going to be a big part of your marketing game plan. As online customers turn to search engines to find information and content before making a purchase, organic search has become an essential marketing channel: 93% of online experiences begin with a search engine.[4] A SEO

---

4 https://www.imforza.com/blog/8-seo-stats-that-are-hard-to-ignore/.

specialist can not only help you rank your website better, but also help you discover new opportunities. The SEO specialist will provide recommendations and guidance for content strategies to increase organic traffic to your site.

SEO strategists handle a number of responsibilities, including:

- Tracking and developing campaigns.

- Determining target keywords and analyzing data based on how users are discovering what you offer.

- Understanding your audience and communicating these audience trends.

- Promoting content.

- Finding new opportunities within search engine results pages.

- Auditing changes made by development for possible SEO downsides, and analyzing analytics and reports. (If your ranking on Google goes down, you need to tweak your SEO to get you back on track. By looking at conversion rates of keywords, you can identify why you are going down.)

4. **Content/Community Manager:** If Google is king, then content is the queen, prince/princess, and probably court jester of your marketing portfolio. Having an exceptional writer on your staff is a must if you plan to have a website, publish a blog, participate in social media, offer long-form content, do PR, or advertise. (In other words, if you plan to do marketing.)

Once you have a strong writer in place, you can look at hiring freelancers to supplement and help you scale the quantity of content. Content is a valuable company asset, and this position is the voice of your business by promoting your content to relevant and targeted audiences. They create new content and find ways to repurpose content for different media and advertising campaigns.

The skills needed to grow and develop your online communications are:

- Ability to identify the audience(s) you want to target.

- Genuine delight in engaging people in conversations.

- Finesse in asking questions to learn more about a customer's needs/identify their greatest interest.

- Solid grasp of company brand identity.

- Patience.

- Professional communication skills.

- Ability to deliver quick, thoughtful responses.

- Ability to recognize leads in conversations and set up meetings.

5. **Paid Search Role:** The paid search role, or PPC specialist, is often outsourced to agencies, but more and more companies are taking this role in-house. This person is your return-on-investment (ROI) time-traveler. While some content and SEO campaigns can take months to drive revenue, paid search and other

advertising channels can often create a much-shorter timeline to ROI.

When hiring a PPC or paid search specialist, look for individuals with strong financial backgrounds who understand return on ad spend and how businesses operate on a cash basis. Here's a sample checklist that a PPC team uses on a daily basis:

- Ask consultant if client is making money or getting quality leads each week.

- Review spending and make sure it's on budget.

- Check for conversions and optimize keywords and landing page.

- Review Quality Scores.

- Add new keywords and determine negative keywords (ones that don't resonate with customers) so you can cancel, or at least pause, losing ads.

- Check ad copy performance, and adjust and write new ad copy.

- Make bid adjustments.

- Analyze landing-page results from radical split tests.

- Launch new campaigns or tests.

- Write weekly PPC updates.

6. **Social Media Manager:** Social media platforms like Instagram, Facebook, Twitter, Pinterest, and Snapchat are great places to introduce your business to new audiences and make sales, so you need a

social media manager to curate your brand's social channels. Posting content is important, but you also need a social media manager to monitor and respond to comments since so many consumers also use social media for customer service. Don't forget — if your audience is active on social media, you need a social media manager right there as well.

Social media isn't just a place where people share silly GIFs and photos of their kids. It's a place where your brand can promote your own content (and some curated content) to engage with your audience on a personal level.

It's also a high-stakes customer service channel. If people aren't happy with your social customer service, it could drive away some of your existing customers and won't help you bring in new ones.

A customer-centric social manager could be one of your best customer retention assets.

The duties include:

- Creating a social media strategy.
- Proposing budgets for your social media activities.
- Managing social media campaigns and change.
- Creating and uploading posts, images, and videos.
- Monitoring, analyzing, and evaluating your social media campaigns and strategies.
- Monitoring trends in social media.

7. **Analyst:** The marketing world has undergone several changes in recent years, but the most important development is an obvious one: the rise of Big Data. Businesses have started to adopt data-driven strategies to inform their marketing initiatives. Recent statistics illustrate just how critical data have become to the modern marketing team:

- 64% of marketing executives "strongly agree" that data-driven marketing is crucial to success in a hypercompetitive global economy.[5]

- 66% of marketing leaders have seen an increase in new customers as a result of data-driven initiatives.

- 63% of marketers reported that their spending on data-driven marketing and advertising grew over the last year.[6]

Of course, a single employee can't handle the entire implementation of a data-driven marketing strategy. That requires the input and cooperation of the entire organization, from senior executives down to individual team members. But a data-driven team does need members who specialize in data analysis and can contextualize data to fit their business's objectives.

5   https://www.forbes.com/sites/forbespr/2015/11/03/new-report-shows-data-driven-marketing-crucial-for-success-in-hyper-competitive-global-economy/#7d3b8b8a65dd.

6   https://www.mediamath.com/blog/resource/the-global-review-data-driven-marketing-and-advertising/#sthash.YxrsCjSA.dpuf.

Data-driven marketing strategies yield several benefits for your marketing team, all of which a data analyst can help facilitate.

8. **Brand Manager:** Modern marketers leverage many different channels to reach customers, which has made today's marketing landscape more competitive than ever before. It's increasingly important to develop a recognizable and trustworthy brand. Consider these statistics:[7]

- It takes an average of five to seven impressions before someone will remember your brand.

- Business-to-business (B2B) brands that connect with buyers on an emotional level earn twice the impact than brands that sell business or functional value.

- B2B decision-makers consider the brand a central element of a supplier's value proposition.

Unfortunately, many businesses fail to create a distinct brand vision or strategy. They simply rely on their combined marketing efforts to naturally build a strong brand. But as branding becomes more important to B2B and B2C buyers, businesses must prioritize initiatives that contribute to brand-building and awareness.

A brand manager is responsible for shaping the image and reputation of your business among your target audience. This role leverages a combination of

---

7   https://www.protocol80.com/blog/b2b-branding-statistics.

customer feedback, market research, and competitive analysis to assess the status of a business in an industry. From there, a brand manager defines and implements a branding strategy throughout all marketing functions, from content creation to design to PR.

9. **Outside Expert/Architect:** An expert architect sees the big picture. They listen to and interpret company business goals and thoughtfully educate and guide the players through the process. They glean the most potential out of a marketing plan and interpret company aspirations.

Architects are trained problem-solvers. The value of an expert architect lies in their pragmatic ability to balance design, construction, and cost. With an expert architect in place, your marketing efforts become more fluid, and you achieve desired results more quickly.

The expert architect position in your winning modern marketing team can be thought of as someone who ensures *marketing compliance*: an overseer of a less formal audit component that makes sure your time, effort, and budget are spent wisely.

Go for One Big Goal

Once you have found your team, it's time to focus on a common team goal; you need a bridge between creating the team and being able to track their success in accomplishing goals. Doing so requires setting and paying attention to goals (often thought of as quotas). Be realistic in terms of what you expect from your new hires and employees; it may take time for them to adapt to your business and marketing plan.

Tracking your team's marketing performance guarantees a smooth transition for both current and new reps. "Stack" your team members side by side to make sure everyone is on the same page in terms of performance. Keeping an eye on your marketing analytics can help detect bottlenecks and other problems that could be holding your team back.

If your marketing organization isn't productive, how can you realistically expect to scale? Productivity is about maximizing your time and tasks within a reasonable time frame. Priorities vary depending on whom you ask. A healthy knowledge of productivity tools shows that you're motivated and skilled at time management. Popular tools include Slack, Trello, Google Drive, and Dropbox.

Too often, people assume that you should only focus on one thing in your life, period, but that's not what this strategy is about. It's about being smart about what you pursue. Yes, you can achieve a lot of things ... just not at the same time. You can't build a career, get in shape, compete in marathons, write a book, invest in a business, have kids, *and* travel the world all at once, but you *can* do all those things over a lifetime. (See Figure 1.4: Focus and Success.)

Just understand that when there's no structure, there's chaos. The natural thing for most people is to start setting goals or picking one priority to focus on, but unless you have *trained* your mind to focus on one thing, it's not a smart thing to do.

Scaling up a business with a strong marketing component does require that you are able to set, focus on, and accomplish your goals. That is part of having that scaleur's growth mindset. As a business owner, to accomplish these goals, you may have to go from "I want everything" to "I appreciate what I have." It is about controlling your desires in order to achieve a greater outcome.

Figure 1.4: Focus and Success

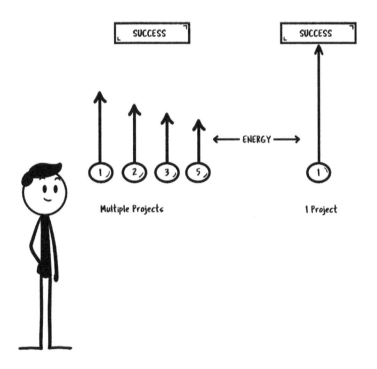

Instead of having lots of small goals that are mostly meaningless, go for a few big goals that matter. Try knocking off one every few months or even one a year if you have to. My current goal is to pivot my career in a new direction. Then straight after that, I'm going to knock off some big speeches to up my public speaking game. Other than those two items, that's about it. This strategy puts the primary focus on only one or two goals, so you get results faster. You may find that as you gain momentum and see results quickly, you don't need motivation to reach that one big goal — your results become your motivation, and they require all your energy and focus.

Not yet convinced? Take these two-minute tests:

- Test 1
  - Set your alarm for 1 minute.
  - Write out the alphabet from A to Z, followed by the numbers 1 through 9, as many times as you can.
  - Example: a, b, c, d, e ... z, 1, 2, 3 ... 9, a, b ...
  - How many characters did you draw?
- Test 2
  - Set your alarm for 1 minute again.
  - Alternate writing the sequential letters and numbers.
  - Example: a, 1, b, 2, c, 3 ...
  - How many characters did you draw this time?

I bet you have fewer characters in Test 2, right? It has been proven that multitasking is hard to master, because you have a lot of interruptions. Focus on one thing, and do it right. Apply this same principle when scaling up your marketing. Find that one goal, and track your teams as they move toward achieving it.

Chapter Review

It's time to think about some important key questions that will reveal how ready you are to scale up your company. Use the tables below to answer Yes or No to see how ready you are to scale yourself and your A-team, and become a scaleur — to become the entrepreneur who wants to scale up their business and team.

How prepared are you for profitable growth? The following questions will instantly reveal how ready you and your business are to scale up. Just put an X in the column that is most relevant to yourself and your business.

Scale Yourself	Y	N
1. I spend more time working "in" rather than "on" my company.		
2. I would like to invest more time on company development.		
3. I have a network of other entrepreneurs whom I regularly ask for advice.		
4. I am not getting tired of running and expanding my company.		
5. I can be out of the office for three weeks without anything going wrong.		
6. I have a good work-life balance.		
7. I am happy.		
8. I regularly attend external or internal courses.		
9. I want to scale my own life.		

If you put an X for everything in the Y column, you are a scaleur!

If not, it is time to start setting yourself up for success. Think about how you can set yourself up for greater success and scale by selecting three actions you can do differently. Rereading the chapter about growth mindset is a good start.

Scale Your Team	Y	N
1. We are usually able to hire employees within our allocated time frames.		
2. We have an onboarding program for new employees.		
3. We measure employee satisfaction at least once a year.		
4. For every change in the company, we ask if and how the customer is affected.		
5. I would rehire every current employee with enthusiasm.		
6. We use outsourcing and/or offshoring for (part of) our operations.		
7. We have formulated core values.		
8. We have an open culture and communication.		
9. All marketing team members have clear annual goals and a plan to achieve them.		

If your answers lean to the "Y" column, it means you are ready to start scaling.

RuLe 2

Ensure Your Strategy Is Scalable

Growing to scale will put your business under more pressure than ever before. It's not the time to gloss over issues and assume the kinks will work out as you grow. Take a closer look at every variable: infrastructure, operations, systems, products, services, and — especially — your budget.

If there are any weaknesses in the way your business runs today, scaling will only magnify them. Set aside the time to turn your business inside out and make sure you can truly support sudden growth. Before you even consider how to scale, your marketing should already run like a well-oiled machine.

Scale back before you scale up. Examine your current processes to see where you can streamline, and determine which marketing efforts are generating a positive ROI. You have to audit what is taking place and where the strengths and weaknesses are. Being able to scale successfully means knowing what attracts and retains the customers you've already acquired and leveraging that knowledge for growth that's sustainable. Identify process gaps that already exist and come up with strategies to address these before they turn into process chasms that cause you immense problems farther down the line. If something isn't working with 10 staff and 50 customers, how will you cope with 100 staff and 5,000 customers?

It is time to take a hard look inside your business to see if you are ready for growth. You can't know what to do differently unless you take stock of where your business stands today. Try to think of everything. You'll need to do some hard thinking and research to come up with proper cost estimates, but doing so will improve your plan. Spend time looking at the marketing systems and processes that are working for you, as well as those that aren't, because extra strain will be felt across the board. Cut back on what's not working. If you are scaling up, it's time to get serious about processes.

Consider the next example. Scaling your business obviously assumes you will get more inbound leads, which lead to more calls, which can lead to more sales. Do you have the structure in place to generate more leads and sales from end to end? Do you have:

- A sufficient lead flow to generate the desired number of leads?
- Marketing systems to track and manage leads?
- Enough sales representatives to follow up and close leads?
- A robust system to manage sales orders?
- A billing system and receivables function for follow-up to ensure invoices are collected on a timely basis?

Not all marketing programs are scalable. Some channels are just too small to make a significant difference for your business over the long term. Others may work on a small scale, but as soon as you pump more money into them, all you see is your costs going up. Just because some platforms, like LinkedIn, Facebook, Instagram, or Twitter, are working, it does not mean they will work when you start adding to the budget. *The only way to know for sure is to test.* Identify those channels or campaigns that are working, and slowly add to the budget over time. If you see that your acquisition costs are relatively steady, that means you have found something scalable.

Take Google, which has clearly demonstrated this concept by adding customers at a quick pace while adding very few additional resources to serve those customers, which is why they were able to increase their margin at a rapid rate in just a few short years. Or consider Microsoft, whose initial costs for developing an advertising platform or operating system are high, but once it is on the market, they can sign up users or sell multiple copies of the related software with minimal cost increases.

These tech companies do share another commonality that makes scalability easier to achieve: They have low operating overhead and little to no burden of warehousing and inventory, and they don't need a lot of resources or infrastructure to grow rapidly.

Some businesses are easier to scale than others. A truly scalable business is one that keeps low marginal costs while increasing revenue and works efficiently with less involvement from the business owner. Here are some examples:

- **Software:** A classic and obvious sample of a scalable business. Once the product is ready, additional copies can be released with minimal extra cost. By adding monthly recurring revenues to your pricing model, you will set yourself up for sustainable growth. For example, you could let customers buy your service every month, at a rate per user. They will use the software and you will have a monthly income stream.

- **Social media:** Facebook, Twitter, Instagram, LinkedIn. It seems like any new platform for sharing photos and impressions is welcomed. Social media platforms/apps help with reaching lots of people or potential customers. You can share pictures, testimonials, videos about your company, etc., to generate customer interaction. This will maximize your online presence, which will help you go farther in scaling up.

- **Downloads:** The scalability of digital music, books, games, and applications is similar to software's scalability. An app, once launched, can be downloaded thousands of times a day. A white paper can be created once and added to a website landing page for downloading. More and more people will pay for such products, but you only have to put time and energy into creating them once.

- **E-commerce and events:** Any product or service provided via the internet is scalable. Because of their digital (and hence easily reproducible) nature, information business, webinars, and many kinds of consulting services can be delivered to a mass of people using only a computer's camera and microphone and an inexpensive program such as Zoom, Skype, FaceTime, etc. Potential and current customers subscribe to attend a webinar and pay a fee for it. You only spend an hour or two to create the event, and profit from hosting it.

- **Line production and franchising:** Most processes of line commodity production are automated. The net cost is relatively low (although you always must keep an eye on the quality). Never let down client expectations — that would undermine their loyalty. When a person comes to McDonald's, they want the same Big Mac they had the previous time. Ray Kroc set a standard down to the smallest specifications, including weight, sauce amount, and fat content in every burger. You can set similar standards for your business that make it both manageable and scalable.

Can You Create a Flexible Strategic Roadmap?

Now that you have the first insights or foundations for scaling (what you need to start to scale up) and you've evaluated the marketing for your business from top to bottom, it's time to start building your roadmap. It's very much like taking a family road trip: You need a map of where you're going before you start gassing up the car. The marketing roadmap for your business has to include the milestones that you want to achieve at reasonable intervals: Here's when we hire a digital marketing manager; here's when we expand our marketing efforts. It should also be flexible enough to accommodate the unknown and unexpected.

Keep your scaling roadmap at the forefront of every decision you make. If a new move or decision doesn't contribute to hitting your strategic milestones, don't spend money just because you can. Remember: Every decision you make while learning how to scale your business should be aimed at building long-term growth. Keep checking in monthly to evaluate whether revenue is on track, your operating costs are staying low, and your teams are achieving key initiatives.

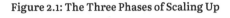

Figure 2.1: The Three Phases of Scaling Up

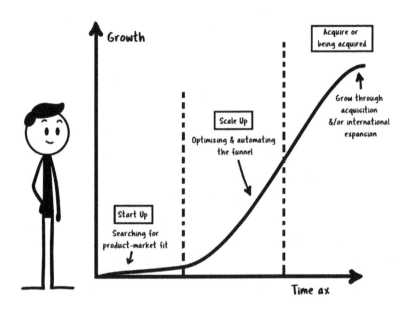

There are three main phases to scaling up (see Figure 2.1: The Three Phases of Scaling Up) that you can use as touchstones for progress. In Phase 1, you start a company and make sure you have a product fit. In Phase 2, once you have the right product market fit and you have scalable systems, scaleurs, a strategy, and a success panel in place, with a steady income stream, it is time to start to scale up. Finally, in Phase 3, you acquire a new business, you are acquired by another larger company, and/or you expand internationally.

Once you pass the startup phase, it is time to build your roadmap to success and your scalable strategy. When I start at a company, I start drafting the marketing strategy plan, based on three parts.

1. What is the current blueprint? What does the company have as of today in terms of:

- Tags and Pixels — do we have the right tracking systems in place and can we trust the data? Tags will help personalize, target, track, analyze, and report on data/performance of visitors to our website.

- Website Performance — is the website optimized enough to convert leads into customers?

  - How we are ranking in Google? How do customers find us?

  - Once at the website, how easy is it for prospective customers to navigate it and find their way? Do we have the right content, and do we bond with them?

  - How can we become friends with our visitors and convert them into customers once they fill in the contact fields?

- Email Marketing — email is still the #1 communication channel. Do we have an email plan in place? What does our lead magnet — something we give for free in exchange for contact details — look like?

- Social Media — are we putting our message where our audience hangs out most of every day? Are we using it for both organic (free) and paid advertising?

- PPC (pay per click) — are we using paid tactics to gain visibility? Do we have the right keywords in place to be found on the web?

- Dashboard — how do we visualize our results to make better decisions?

2. What are the must-win battles you want to achieve in a given year? What are the success drivers you want to see at the end of a successful year? Thinking about whether you have a great foundation in place. Plan to increase the customer experience by X% and grow your leads by Y%.

3. Draw up a plan with milestones of what to achieve by when. This will make your objectives as smart as possible. Set them for a whole year, but cut them into monthly and even weekly goals to make them easier to manage and achieve.

Setting up a digital strategy roadmap is one thing to do, but you also must understand your organization as a whole: What is the budget for your team? What are the strengths and weaknesses of the company and where do you want to focus when scaling up? What do your customers need and how can you delight them?

Is Your Marketing Budget in Order?

It takes money to make money — but how much makes the difference between simple growth and scaling smart. Scaling should be a calculated investment that your marketing can support, and not just by breaking even. Is the demand actually there to validate scaling now? Will you be able to bring in the leads you need without exceeding costs? Can your budget handle the new infrastructure/systems or employees that will be needed to support your expansion?

Keep in mind that 82% of businesses that fail do so because of cash flow problems.[8] To scale successfully, you'll need financing. Show your strategic roadmap to your board, and demonstrate how the business will be able to grow to scale, with measurable goals tied to profit and revenue along the way.

Going from being an employee at Unibake, a global corporation worth $1.3 billion, to consulting with CHD Expert, a company worth around $7.5 million, included going from a marketing budget where I could learn and try things to one that was very tight and where each penny was counted. However, as the saying goes, bigger is not necessarily better. Scaling up requires letting go of many of the little things that eat up your time, and that's harder to do in a larger firm.

The smaller size of a company requires narrowing scope and focus more precisely on the target market (channels, countries, audience, etc.) where you would be most effective. That can mean doing more with less. In practical terms, that can mean, for example, working hard to churn out five high-quality, high-impact posts rather than a scattershot output of 15 that are general or of lower quality.

Despite the disparity in size and approaches between the two firms where I worked, the rule remained the same:

---

8   https://smallbiztrends.com/2019/03/startup-statistics-small-business. html.

Prepare your plan and create your list of what is essential. As you go along, run through your list regularly and ask yourself again whether you really need to incur certain costs to carry out that plan.

The leaner, meaner, and better calibrated your processes are, the better positioned you are to scale.

To-Do

Make a list of your must-have vs. nice-to-have plan elements. Read it again, and write down what the gain will be in a quantitative way if you buy a given tool. Put the numbers behind it and only go for the tools that deliver you the most leads and the best road toward achieving your goals.

Know Your Strengths and Differentiators

When it comes to identifying a competitive edge, a lot of entrepreneurs give into preconceived notions of where they want their marketing business to go, but as their businesses scale, they begin to understand their market and products better. A lot of entrepreneurs/scaleurs will be challenged personally and professionally, and perhaps even be put in compromising positions that make them question themselves and their beliefs. Introspection can keep us motivated and help us push for our dreams. It's good to have high self-esteem and self-regard, but we also must be realistic in what we want to achieve.

For example, at some point, a marketer — whether the owner of a business that provides marketing services or a member of the marketing department of another type of business — will figure out that they are better at providing after-sales email services than general content writing. That marketer will then focus on maintaining staff and specializing in the tools needed to provide after-sales email services instead of writing generic content. That can provide the reality check that strengthens the business in general and its marketing process in particular.

Identify your top two or three differentiators — the factors that make your business unique — so you can use them to stand out in a sea of competitors. Competitive differentiation is a process that helps buyers distinguish your firm from similar ones and gives them a compelling reason to select you.

You don't have to be radically different from your competitors (although if you are, so much the better). Rather, you need to find something about your business that you can own and make a distinctive part of your brand. To engage with your clientele, you have to provide and promote differentiators that they care about.

There are multiple ways to find out what your customers really think to find your differentiators and where your customers think you stand out.

1. **Create a short survey.** The areas you want to focus on are improving the customer experience, product and service satisfaction, and what inspires customers to come back and refer friends. As you craft 10 to 12 short questions, keep in mind that they should lead to answers you can't easily get in person or online.

2. **Analyze your marketing results.** Customers leave behind digital breadcrumbs that offer insights into what they want. In email, look at your open and click-through rates to see which content strikes a chord and

what's falling flat. Most of the popular social media networks offer free insights into performance, so take advantage of Facebook Insights, Twitter Analytics, and other such tools to see how you're doing.

3. **Ask customers how you're doing.** When customers are at the cash register or come to your website on a regular basis, don't be afraid to ask for feedback. When you do, be explicit by letting them know that you're looking to grow your business and would love their honest feedback about what you can do to improve their experience and keep them coming back to your company.

4. **Get internal feedback.** A lot of knowledge is in the brains of your colleagues. Ask them questions and challenge them to help you make your marketing better.

5. **True differentiation takes place in the mind.** It happens when a person connects your firm with an idea; when they think to themselves, "Ah! [Your company name here] — they're the firm that's known for _____." If your prospects fill in the blank with something that's both relevant to their businesses and not associated with your competitors, then you have created a powerful competitive differentiator.

Armed with this information, you're ready to put a plan in place that not only scales your marketing, but also scales your business. Since repetition is the key to remembering, reiterate your main differentiators in your social media profiles, website, and newsletters.

A matrix can help you determine your differentiators. In the columns, list your competitors; in the rows, enumerate the differentiators. Here are ways that businesses find their strengths and turn them into differentiators:

1. **Focus:** Maybe your company has a global foodservice operator data set. Lots of competitors have a global database (not dedicated to foodservice) or foodservice data for certain regions.

2. **Simplicity:** Your competitors might have elaborate, fancy websites, but some are hard to navigate, and it can be difficult to understand what they offer. Keep it simple and logical — this makes it easy to convert leads. Use only one call to action on the landing page instead of 10.

3. **Scalability:** Maintain a focus on the things that can be scaled up by providing access to a monthly data set such as recurring revenues.

To-Do

Make a matrix to demonstrate where your company stands out, and where you should be focusing when writing content, branding your company, and undertaking other important tasks that contribute to scaling the business.

Delight Your Customers

Customer delight happens when you surprise a customer (or client) by exceeding their expectations. When you meet expectations, you have customer satisfaction. When you exceed expectations, you achieve customer delight. You accomplish this by listening to your customers and their needs. We care because there is something to be said for word-of-mouth marketing, and delighted customers will tell other potential customers about your business. It will take time to identify your ideal customer, but this step — and its inevitable mistakes — will move your business toward sustainable growth and devoted customers.

Attract, convert, close, and delight: We know from HubSpot that these are core pillars of the traditional inbound marketing strategy[9] (see Figure 2.2: Conversion Funnel). It's easy to get caught up in the attract process, creating content for lead generation. It's important to attempt to reach the convert and close stages and see those leads turn into customers. But are you remembering the importance of the delight stage in your marketing strategy? Success in scaling is not just about customer satisfaction, but about creating a powerful emotional reaction that results in happy customers who want to continue using your company and become your best promoters.

---

9   https://www.hubspot.com/inbound-marketing.

Figure 2.2: Conversion Funnel

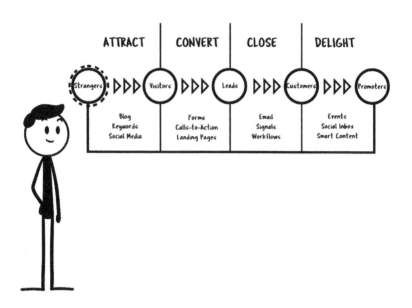

Do You Understand Your Customers' Needs?

When developing content, for your website, your blog, or through social media networks, you have to listen to customer needs, so you must design this content with the customer in mind. Social media and blog content comprise the attract stage of your marketing strategy, leading to the ability to convert leads. Delight should be present in each stage, beginning when they are still visitors through to the customer stage and never actually ending. Social media networks and blogs allow you to interact with your visitors, delighting them through multiple channels and ensuring that visitors view you as a trusted advisor.

A delighted customer is a customer who would circle a "totally satisfied" option on a survey. According to Hughes and Company, "totally" satisfied customers have a repurchase rate that is three to 10 times higher than "somewhat" satisfied customers. A delighted customer will be happy to reuse your business and to recommend it to their family and friends. Referral leads convert roughly 30% better than leads generated from other marketing channels.[10] Focusing on delighting your customers in your marketing strategy can increase your revenue and improve your relationship with your customers, which leads to referrals and social sharing, as well as an increase in customer retention and loyalty.

When I was an export manager at Unibake, one of the key things we did to scale the department was to focus on delighting the customers. The customers in this case were not individuals but foodservice distributors, retailers, and sister companies, but even though we were working with high-budget entities, individualized attention was just as crucial.

We had three bakeries mass-producing baked goods in Belgium. We would give customers tours of the factory (including a chat with the chef), followed by dinner in the evening. Over several days, we'd spend a lot of time with representatives of the companies and get to know them on a personal level.

We also repeated this approach in our visits to customers on their home turf. For example, we were persistent in pursuing Ledo Croatia as a new client. To woo them, I visited Croatia several times. I got to know the point person there on a personal level. As time went on, she told us about her wedding and later sent a notice about her pregnancy — clear signs that although we had a business relationship, there was an undercurrent of friendship that had helped us seal the deal.

---

10 https://www.hughesandco.ca/blog/why-your-marketing-strategy-needs-to-focus-on-customer-delight.

These kinds of "delight the customer" practices are enormously helpful in scaling a business or its marketing department because they help bring in more business and deeper loyalties. The personal touch is not scalable — you may need to meet with each individual customer in person — but you can automate and standardize the process of how many customer visits you make through the samples you take along and a basic agenda for every presentation. Doing so will win time by making it easy and efficient to repeat the processes. Once in a while, you could enhance the personal aspect by holding a group customer demo session.

4 Principles for Identifying Your Ideal Customer

1. **Provide real-time support.** Have you ever thought about how your customers feel about spending time waiting on hold in a phone queue?

   Does it really have any worth to say, "*Your call is important to us*"? An American Express survey found that the maximum amount of time customers are willing to wait is 13 minutes.[11] Your customer expectations align with reality when your business adopts new technology to provide real-time support to your customers. That puts customer experience on pace to exceed price and product as the number-one differentiator for companies.

   Great customer experience can be achieved by using live-chat software and engagement tools that boost

---

11 https://www.icmi.com/resources/2017/what-do-customers-really-think-about-long-wait-times.

customer satisfaction rates. Live chat has been found to be preferred over other communication channels, such as phone and email — the real-time support it delivers to customers makes it popular. Ecoconsultancy reports that 79% of customers prefer live chat because of the immediacy it offers compared to other channels.[12] Consumers just want answers as quickly as possible and are often too busy, or even too lazy, to navigate your website.

Live chat connects you with your customers instantly and lets you address their issues in real time. It triggers proactive chat messages to guide customers in their buying journey and improve their experience with your business.

2. **Analyze customer feedback.** "A satisfied customer is the best business strategy of all," says international management expert and bestselling author Michael LeBoeuf. Customer feedback is the core of any business and one of the main factors in growth. It is the one thing that gives a business a clearer view of how it is doing. Collecting feedback requires asking customers to share their opinions about the product, service, or overall experience with your business. The right moment to ask for feedback is right after a customer service conversation.[13] You are already in a

---

12 https://econsultancy.com/consumers-prefer-live-chat-for-customer-service-stats/.

13 https://www.revechat.com/blog/how-to-ask-for-customer-feedback/.

conversation with the customer, so it feels natural to ask for feedback.

CHD operates in the foodservice industry. During the COVID-19 pandemic, the landscape of this industry totally changed, and so too did customer interests and demands. It was necessary to conduct a survey asking about the inconveniences brought about by the disruption of the pandemic. Surprised by the results, we had to change our direction. What really counted was that our customers appreciated that we took their pain and hardship into consideration.

You think you know your customer because you speak with them and their colleagues regularly, but do you truly understand their needs? During these turbulent times, CHD made an effort to understand the main problems our customers were experiencing — without trying to sell them our products. That resonated with them.

To do this, we called or emailed our five top accounts and asked, "What will be the main pain your company will see after the COVID?" We did this without linking it to a company offer. Based on the feedback, we created a survey that incorporated their responses to gauge the impact on the rest of our customers. As a result, we discovered we had to go back to our foundations. Instead of selling an advanced lead-scoring model, we had to return to the basics: just data.

3. **Personalize your communications.** Today's customers expect business interactions to be customized to

their needs and preferences. They get frustrated when they receive information that doesn't resonate, especially when it comes from trusted advisors.

With the right technology to collect customer data and turn it into actionable insights, you can personalize each customer interaction and provide unique messaging for each of your clients regardless of their preference in channels.

Start with the basics: Make a list divided between your top 10 customers and your prospects to create dedicated emails to send to those groups. That way, you avoid sending products or services to customers who are already buying your products or services.

If you know that 20% of your top customers drive 80% of your revenue, it's good business to send them something special. At Unibake, we took the time to do the little things that can set a company apart in a crowded industry: efforts such as sending customers comfy and cozi "hygge" socks during the holidays (a Danish tradition) or a thank you postcard can achieve miracles. It shows customers they are genuinely appreciated. An old-fashioned gesture of gratitude never goes out of style.

4. **Solve one problem for one customer.** People don't buy products; they buy solutions to problems. Startups can't hope to solve all the problems for a whole market — and they shouldn't want to. For a startup, the opportunity to narrowly focus on one specific problem and build the perfect solution

to that problem is an advantage that must be exploited.

Startups have the ability to zero in on one problem for a very specific, small, and defined audience. Don't try to "boil the ocean" right out of the gate with a mass-market product (unless, of course, you think competing with massive companies on a level playing field is a good strategy).

Remember:

- Facebook started by focusing on one dorm at Harvard.
- Mailchimp was created to design emails for the clients of one design consultancy.
- Shopify started as a shopping cart solution for a snowboarding website.
- Groupon was created for one office building in Chicago.

If you're aiming small, your laser-focused launch is only going to require one rocket — but that rocket has to showcase one awesome attribute. Trying for more than one product or service will drain important resources and will distract from the necessary process of perfecting your number-one offering. Such a lack of focus is also a tell-tale warning sign for investors.

Perfecting your one killer rocket means ensuring it has something that lifts it far above your competition, so you'd be smart to focus on giving one product something special. In the beginning, you are better off doing one thing really well and focusing on that one thing; later, you'll be able to use customer feedback to add new features and broaden your market reach.

Case in point: Most people think that consumers want choice. The reality is consumers don't want choice; they want *freedom from* choice. If you can solve one problem proficiently for a customer with one simple feature, those consumers telling all their friends is the only marketing you'll need.

One thing I've learned over the years is that you not only have to sell one thing at a time; you have to sell a solution rather than a product. CHD, the global foodservice database provider, doesn't sell data. We sell the solution that companies can increase their market share. By accessing the database, they have access to millions of new leads they can start targeting, so their market share will increase as well.

To-Do

Do you really understand your customers? If not, draft a survey with about eight questions to ask your customers about your performance — and always include something for the customer. Why should they spend five minutes of their time? Offer a discount, a check, a free book ...

Chapter Review

Make your company blueprint (where you stand right now), think about your must-win battles for a successful year, and draw up your first monthly plan to achieve your goals.

Identify your competitive edge (what sets your business apart from your competitors) and your customers' needs (what you can deliver to those customers that they want), and understand the core strengths of your business so you can invest in focused growth.

These key principles will allow your marketing team to understand what your customer really wants from your business. Also, it's good practice to look at the growth of your business from the perspective of your customers. Your internal team must maintain focus and set milestones for the growth of the business.

Once you've identified your ideal customer, build a marketing funnel that orbits around your needs as a business (i.e., a prospect fills out a form on your website, your marketing team immediately schedules a demo, and the prospect becomes a customer) and study your buyer's behavior. Would your demos be more effective if you had a discovery call first? Is a 90-day sales cycle more realistic for your buyer than 30 days? Consider these things as you're building your funnel.

Take a moment to look at where you stand with these important points.

	Y	N
We have formulated a clear long-term goal for the marketing department (other than financial goals).		
We have formulated measurable annual goals per person.		
We have formulated measurable quarterly and/or monthly goals per person.		
We have a detailed strategic plan.		

We have an effective communications strategy based on customer segmentation.		
We have implemented a growth methodology.		
We receive a monthly budget status report.		
We can express the company's strengths and weaknesses.		
We know our customers' biggest challenges.		
We have sufficient leads in the pipeline.		
We have marketing systems to track and manage leads.		
We have enough sales representatives to follow up on the leads.		
We have the right social media in place for retargeting.		
We know our current blueprint for the company.		
We know the budget.		
We know where we stand vs. the competition.		
We can distinguish must-haves vs. nice-to-have tools.		

Open question: What is your customer's biggest challenge at this moment?

_____

Open question: What are your must-win battles for the year?

_____

Rule 3

Establish Standardized
Systems

You cannot scale your business unless you've established processes and procedures that facilitate streamlined operations. By aligning and standardizing your core functions, you'll be able to quickly build a solid foundation for the long haul. Instead of focusing on short-term fixes, you will be able to accomplish larger business goals with ease.

Before attempting to scale, you must have production processes in place that can easily handle significant increases in the number of leads. That means getting rid of manual processes and replacing them with automated systems that reduce the amount of human work required.

Scaling isn't easy, but once you implement *scalable processes*, you can focus on increasing your leads without wondering whether your marketing department can handle them. *Focus on simplicity and keep customer needs at the core.* If you can check both of those boxes for each scalable process, you're on the right track.

It's time to look at processes you can put in place to maximize your presence to gain recurring revenues.

Scalable Processes to Maximize Your Online Presence

Along with making it simple for existing customers to spread the word about your products or services, you also want to be easily found by new customers. One way to ensure a positive, ubiquitous online presence is to continually update your social media profiles. The more comprehensive they are, including specifics about your location, hours, and prices, the more likely your business is to surface higher in search results. To be sure you show up in all the relevant online directories, take advantage of tools like Single Platform that make it easy to update and populate your online business profile quickly across the web.

Work your local connections. Network with other local small-business owners and entrepreneurs to drive word of mouth, collaborate on joint marketing activities, and stay visible in the neighborhood. All of this elevates your profile as you scale.

Keep an eye on social media. Every new startup is in the public eye. Whatever happens on social media will be examined by the world. It's important in your startup marketing days to watch your social media carefully. Scalability is about surviving as much as it is about growing. If you hit a PR fiasco, you're limiting or even undermining your chance of survival and scalability.

Build your network, because creating the right connections is key to effectively scaling your business and to long-term growth. The mindset that promotes growth and scalability must extend itself to collaborations and partnerships outside the business. Developing a strong PR network is the key to success in the long run. You need a network of collaborations with people and organizations — service providers, sales partners, and suppliers, as well as customers, all of whom may be willing to assist you by providing important market statistics. Such engagements may take the form of formal alliances, and when that happens, scalability becomes achievable with minimum effort.

At CHD, we run a blog and are working with magazines to partner on it. PMQ, a pizza magazine, is one such partner — we have the pizza data, and they have the magazine and the customers. We have also had bloggers reach out to co-write blog posts with us, which boosts both of our followings. We are always looking to combine our expertise with partners in the field. Find your players step by step, and build your network to scale up your business.

Repurposing content is one way to help you with that. It is an approach that takes existing published content, remixes it, and puts a fresh spin on it to create something totally new and wonderfully different. Repurposing content helps with scaling for three main reasons.

1. **Recycling content can help you build your reputation.** Which would you trust more: a business with just a blog, or a business with a blog, an active LinkedIn account, and a well-maintained YouTube channel? Most people would choose the second business. Having an active, wide-reaching presence on the internet establishes your authority and expertise in your field.

2. **Repurposing content helps you connect with your audience.** Some people just don't like reading blog posts. Those same people, though, might enjoy listening to your messages in podcast form on their

commutes. You can tweak your content to appeal to leads at different stages of the sales or marketing funnel, or you can upgrade and repost content for people who may not have seen it the first time around. Repurposing your content can be as helpful for your audience as it is for you.

3. **Repurposing content lets you publish regularly.** How often you publish new content matters almost as much as the quality of that content. Many of the top business bloggers publish once a week, or even more frequently. Recycling your best content in new ways helps you avoid the all-too-common trap of abandoning your blog and other content channels for months at a time when you get busy with other things.

In short, repurposing content helps you get more of the benefits of content marketing with less work. You will save time and effort in creating one piece that you can repurpose to reach more people in much less time than you put into creating it.

15 Clever Ways to Repurpose Your Content: Scale the Replication

While marketing teams are usually most efficient at the campaign level, advanced marketing teams have the capability to clone and replicate entire programs, including workflows and content. Leading marketers devote a portion of their practice to strategically defining best-practice programs, layouts, templates, and more so automation is not a laborious process.

As the number of marketing solutions continues to grow, process and program sustainability will be an increasingly important consideration. Take a critical look at the number of systems required to deliver your multi-channel marketing strategies and seek out platforms that can integrate scalability while delivering personalization throughout the buyer's journey.

If your team is feeling stress from campaign execution, ask which tasks are repetitive for them and don't add value. Centralized campaign execution within a scalable marketing platform delivers unique benefits and efficiencies that help marketers keep pace with new and unique ways to engage with customers.

You can do lot with words on a page. Here are 15 ideas for recycling your written content.

1. **Turn blog posts into podcasts.** One of the simplest ways to repurpose your content is to convert text to audio. Try giving some of your blog posts a second life in the form of podcasts. All you need is a device to record your voice.

   Start by reworking your blog post into a script. You probably won't need to change a lot—just make sure the piece flows smoothly and a listener will be able to follow it easily. If you tend to write in a formal tone, adapt the language in your script to be a little more casual.

   Record yourself reading your script aloud, or hire someone to record it for you. Upload the finished podcast to SoundCloud, BlogTalkRadio, or another hosting site. Don't forget to promote your podcast on social media!

2. **Turn blog posts into white papers.** White papers make great marketing materials, and you can build them out of blog posts. This is an especially good way

to repurpose posts that go into detail about how you solved a problem.

Depending on how in-depth your blog post is, you may need to tweak its structure or add more details to convert it to a white paper. Write a summary for the beginning, and make sure to flesh out the middle with plenty of data to support your points. Once your white paper is done, you can use it as a lead magnet on your site.

You can also choose the best-performing posts on your blog and create a roundup white paper out of them. For instance, with Beacon, you can create a white paper or an ebook from any blog post. The company even claims to have a WordPress (WP) plugin that automatically creates ebooks out of your WP posts. Another great tool that allows you to turn a blog post into a white paper in a matter of minutes is PrintFriendly. It has a Chrome extension that allows you to create a PDF out of any blog post that you read to it.

3. **Make an infographic from content from a blog post.** Do you have any blog posts that are full of shareable statistics and graphs? Pull out those visual-friendly tidbits and make them do double duty as infographics.

You can make infographics on your own with online tools for graphics or video like Canva, Visme, or Animatron Studio. Another option is to hire a professional designer to do it for you. Keep in mind that whatever route you take, you may want to stick with a single designer so your visual content is consistent.

4. **Update old blog posts with new information.** Skim over your blog archives to look for posts that could benefit from some updates or additions. If you've been blogging for a while, some of your posts probably contain old, outdated information. Expanding old posts with new material is another way to add value without writing whole new posts. To avoid any confusion after you make your changes, add a note to the top of the post letting readers know it's been revised.

   You might have blog posts that are a bit dusty but still very valuable. Update those posts — change them according to the latest numbers and current situation — and you can use them to boost traffic on your blog again. You also could use concepts about national topics and change them to reflect local numbers and data — or vice-versa.

5. **Make a video based on a blog post.** Sometimes video is a better medium than text for explaining things. If some of your blog posts explain complex topics, consider turning them into videos for the visual learners in your audience.

   It's hard to go wrong with any type of video, as long as it's well made. If you're new to videos, though, consider creating a videographic, a whiteboard-style video, or an animated video. These videos are easy to make, and you won't have to get in front of a camera yourself. A tool like wave.video or Lumen5 can help you get started easily.

Many people don't like to read long texts anymore; they want to learn quickly. Videos can showcase complex ideas, products, or services using easily understandable models. For an example, go to Scaleurs.com for the how-to video "Scale in Less Than Two Minutes."

6. **Hold a webinar based on your blog content.** Want to attract more leads and interact with your existing audience in real time? Holding a webinar is a good way to do that. If you have a back catalog of blog posts, it's easy to come up with webinar content by turning blog content into presentation slides. Mix things up by combining information from a couple of posts that are related to each other and add a little brand-new content.

At CHD, we decided to hold a webinar for the European market during the COVID-19 pandemic. The market was changing and so was the industry. We wanted to inform our customers what they could expect from us in the future. By first conducting a survey in three countries, we asked for feedback on consumer habits — specifically, if and how they would change post-COVID when visiting restaurants. It should be easy to gather 150 to 200 people to chat about your industry — and delight them further by including them in a conversation.

7. **Publish your writing on LinkedIn and Medium.** Why confine your best writing to your blog when it could reach thousands more readers on big sites like LinkedIn and Medium? The more places people can discover your content, the better. There's a catch,

though. If Google thinks you're posting your content in multiple places to game the SEO system, they could penalize you, so it's important to republish your work the right way. Here's how you can avoid incurring SEO penalties:

- Be selective about which pieces you publish on sites other than your own blog. Broadcast the ones with the most mass appeal as widely as you can, and keep the more niche pieces on your own site.

- Publish only an excerpt from each post. Add a link to your own blog for people who want to read the whole thing.

- Avoid posting the same content word for word. Make some changes to the text before republishing on Medium or LinkedIn.

- Wait at least a couple of weeks before reposting any content, so Google has time to index the original version on your site.

At Marketing Scaleurs, we decided to work with Medium as a reference point — a good source for being seen and getting information.

8. **Answer questions on the web through live chat.** On discussion boards like Quora and Reddit, your blog posts can double as answers to people's questions. Keep an eye out for questions and conversations that are relevant to blog posts you've written, and publish excerpts of your work that address those topics — but only do this if your content is actually applicable. Whenever we publish a new blog post, we search

Quora for related questions, submit a helpful answer, and add a link to our new blog post if it's relevant and brings more value.

This tip works in reverse, too: If you've written any original, cogent answers to people's questions on discussion boards, see if you can expand those pieces into full blog posts.

Both CHD and Lantmännen decided to implement chatboxes on their websites so visitors could get what they want: answers right away without having to wait. You can do the same.

9. **Combine multiple blog posts into an ebook.** Have you written a lot of blog posts on related topics? Put some of those posts together, and you might find that you've got most of the material for an ebook.

Don't run to Amazon to self-publish your book quite yet, though. Take the time to make your ebook truly high quality. Sequence your posts in a way that makes sense, and edit them to improve the book's flow. Add some fresh, exclusive content so your current readers have an incentive to download the book. Add illustrations, photos, or original research. If you don't know how to format an ebook, hire someone to do it for you. Services like Beacon are great for creating ebooks, even if you don't have a designer.

As discussed previously, you want to nurture customers via a marketing funnel. One way to nurture your customers is to create ebooks to grab their interest. This can work as part of your ladder of value.

10. **Make an audio version of your ebook.** Like blog posts, ebooks are easily converted to audio. You'll have to invest more of your time into recording the book (or spend more to hire a voice professional), but otherwise, the process is mostly the same. Audio content is popular because it lets people multitask. If your average reader tends to be busy, it's smart to provide an audio alternative to your text-based content. Just as with podcasts, head to sites like SoundCloud or BlogTalkRadio to host your audio ebook. It's a great way to leverage your content.

11. **Fill up your email newsletter with content from your blog.** If you send out a weekly or monthly email newsletter, add some excerpts or highlights from your latest blog posts. Include links so people can read the full posts if they're interested. You might see your blog traffic and your email open rate go up with this tactic. Moz is a great example of repurposing content in such a manner. Whenever they have a great new post to share, they post all of it in an email. So much for shorter emails!

    You already have so much valuable content in the form of blog posts and your website. At the same time, email marketing is still one of the most valuable tools for generating leads. Use valuable existing content you know is working. Just tweak your blog or web posts, and put the result in an email. It's a great way to keep up the momentum of your contact with customers.

12. **Put your presentations on SlideShare.** Have you given a presentation or hosted a webinar lately? Don't just let your slides languish in a dark corner of your hard

drive — they can keep working for you. Go over your deck and make sure all the information it contains is evergreen (timeless). Then upload the deck to SlideShare, where anyone can find and view it.

13. **Use visual content on Pinterest and/or Instagram.** To really extend the life of your images, put them on Pinterest. Most social media posts fade away within a few days or even a few hours, but "pins" can last for months. Infographics, image-based how-to guides, and photos that represent your brand are all good choices for Pinterest. Instagram is another visual social media platform where you can repost your images, although Instagram posts don't last as long as pins.

A lot of end consumers are using Instagram, but if yours is a B2B company, I would recommend putting more effort and budget into your LinkedIn channel rather than your Instagram channel. Also, Instagram stories tend to be more successful than Instagram posts. Decide on the main channels where you want to be found, and make sure the content is relevant.

14. **Create an online course based on your old content.** If you've ever created a series of how-to articles, videos, or webinars, consider repackaging them into a course. Online courses are a perfect way to scale up your business. As with ebooks, you'll probably want to sprinkle in some new content so longtime readers will want to sign up. Even a short, free course can help you get more email subscriptions. Platforms like Udemy allow you to host your courses for free. Other options include Stepik and Teachable. You

can even host your course on YouTube! Just create a separate playlist for that, and get ready to grow your audience.

15. **Use your data.** If you've done any kind of original research or testing, don't discard the data when you're finished. Turn the results into an infographic, a case study, or another type of content that highlights your findings. Gathering and making sense of original data is a fantastic way to provide real, unique value.

You probably have more content than you think. With a little creativity, you can turn a single article, blog post, or video into several different pieces of content to use across the web.

Repurposing your content isn't effortless, since you may have to make some edits or add fresh content to what's already there, but it's a lot easier than starting from scratch.

You can decide to use all of these methods, mix and match a handful of options, or try only the strategies with the highest conversion rates. Give yourself deadlines for exploring each tool to determine what works best for you. For example, take two months to try your hand at podcasting, and put some realistic numbers behind it.

Dine2Night, a new food-delivery platform that started in Boston, decided not to opt for Facebook and Instagram platforms as paid social media outlets, since the conversion rates and types of leads were much lower when compared to the leads coming from LinkedIn. Only data will help you to make fact-based decisions without assumptions.

Embrace Automation

Not only should you find the way to maximize your processes.

You also should automate these processes so you can do less work by trusting the machines.

How do you scale without losing the personalization that has resonated with your customers and fueled your current successes? Leveraging marketing automation tools allows you to send highly targeted messages to leads and shorten the marketing cycle. Automated lead nurturing helps you build relationships with customers through helpful emails, follow-ups, social media engagement, etc., to determine when they're truly sales-ready. By automating your creative workflows, you streamline repetitive tasks, cut down on errors, and execute faster.

It's the central puzzle of marketing: sending the right message to the right person at just the right time. As you ramp up your marketing machine by launching simultaneous, complex campaigns, it becomes more and more difficult to do so. To keep up with the complexity and volume of customer and campaign data, you need the right technologies and tools to track, analyze, and optimize your marketing efforts.

Invest in Technology

Technology makes it easier and less expensive to scale a marketing business. You can gain huge economies of scale and more throughput, with less labor, if you invest wisely in technology.

Systems integration is a prime area for improvement in most businesses. Companies today don't run on a single system — they may have a dozen or more, but if those systems don't work together, they create silos, which in turn multiply communication and management problems as your company grows.

In my experience, systems work best when they are integrated with each other. As an example, Dine2Night uses the following three main tools for the nurturing process.

1. **A lead-scoring tool:** Tools like Close tell you what you need to send in a first email message or call so you have consistency and relay the same message regardless of how it goes out. Such a playbook also helps you follow up with your customers. It indicates when and what type of contact your customer needs next, whether it's an email, a phone call, or a LinkedIn message. Everything is automated and there's a tracking function for subsequent contacts.

2. **A nurturing tool:** HubSpot is helpful for inbound leads via paid social media and website conversion, as well as email marketing.

3. **An organizing tool:** Zapier consolidates all the leads in an Excel spreadsheet so you can organize, categorize, and link your follow-ups. As a bonus, it is linked with a lead-generating tool.

One of the most effective ways to ensure consistency in business processes is to automate them, because that eliminates most of the human errors that can affect the scaling of operations. It also cuts down on the amount of time that your staff spends on processes that take them away from their core duties, which in turn can affect morale and lead to other issues when you need to scale operations. However, it's worth paying attention to your marketing infrastructure as well as investing in new software. As you scale your marketing, you will bring in extra staff and ideally attract many more leads, so you have to make sure your processes cover the regular monitoring and upgrading of the infrastructure that supports these areas.

The main takeaway is that you still want to send the right message to your customers, and you want your processes to run smoothly even when your people are switching positions. Data visualization tools and regular testing will help significantly. Here are a few of the tools you'll need in your toolbox (you will find more tools in Part 3).

- **Social media marketing and management tools (organic/free and paid).** Social media marketing is the process of gaining traffic and attention through social media platforms. Your message is different for different audience groups and different channels, so you should have accounts on multiple social media platforms. Some of the most popular networks that can be used in both paid and unpaid marketing are Facebook, YouTube, Twitter, Instagram, LinkedIn, and Tumblr.

- **SEO.** SEO is a measurable, repeatable optimization process that is used to send signals to search engines, notifying them that your site is worth displaying higher up in search results, thereby increasing the amount of organic traffic that your site receives. Search engines use complex algorithms to assess each site in relation to every search that users perform to determine which site should rank best for what users are looking for. Some popular tools include Ahrefs, Google Keyword Planner, Google Console, and Open Site Explorer. By automating your SEO process, you will receive regularly scheduled updates from Google Console that give you an overview of your ranking, including the top search words and conversion rates.

- **Images, design, and video.** People are more likely to engage with posts that contain photos and/or videos because the visual aspect makes posts more interesting to read. Even when you are on a budget, you can do a lot by yourself. Preferred tools include Visme, Piktochart, SlideShare, Adobe Photoshop and Illustrator, Unsplash, and Lumen5. These tools will help you share your message in a uniform and consistent way. Making standardized templates will free up your time, too.

- **Email.** Email marketing isn't new. As long as you're using it right, email is still one of the most valuable and most targeted channels for reaching your audience. Understand open rates, A/B testing, and lead nurturing. Engage the 20% of your customers who will drive 80% of your business. Similarly, instead of creating a design for each and every campaign, your team can agree on a set number of pre-formatted layouts and standard content adaptation rules. Striking a balance between creativity and timely execution can make a huge difference in the number of messages that your limited marketing resources can support.

- **Dynamic content and program tokens.** Tokens, or "merge fields," are system-referenced data points within an automation solution that adjust contact-presented information based on field values. For example, marketers in a certain industry may need personalized content to capture their audience's attention to industry-specific trends. Instead of creating multiple emails, you can reference the data values connected to your marketing database and customize content within the same email, landing page, or any other asset. Popular examples would be Mailchimp or HubSpot.

- **Lead-nurturing tools.** Building a predictable lead-generation machine is challenging. Once you crack this challenge, though, it's extremely rewarding because it can let you scale up faster and be more selective with whom you work with. In the B2B world, most customer relationships begin with content offers, then continue with lead nurturing through the sales funnel. You must understand the full nurturing model and have various types of content (from ebooks to webinars) to serve specific audience needs throughout your funnel. Great tools for this are HubSpot and Marketo.

Automate What You Can, Outsource What You Can't

According to Forbes, 53% of employees believe they can save up to two work hours a day (240 hours per year) through automation, and 78% of business leaders believe that automation can free up to three work hours a day (360 hours per year). That's anywhere from six to nine weeks per year! Automating saves valuable time, but also lets your employees focus their skills on what matters most instead of on repetitive, manual tasks. Activities like employee invoicing, payments, onboarding new clients, responding to new contact requests, and similar routine tasks can be fully automated to help your team focus on critical tasks deserving of their skillsets, without leaving potential customers behind or sacrificing customer service quality.

For what you can't automate, consider outsourcing. Your team may not be able to design a logo or know the ins and outs of SEO, but that doesn't mean you need to hire a full-time graphic designer or SEO marketer. Instead, look to colleagues for recommendations and professional organizations to find freelancers. You'll be able to tap directly into freelancer expertise and skills on an as-needed basis, while saving time and scaling fast.

Similar to outsourcing, more business doesn't necessarily mean more employees. In his book *The Lean Startup*, entrepreneur Eric Ries writes, "It's a really paradoxical thing. We want to think big but start small. And then scale fast. People think about trying to build the next Facebook as trying to start where Facebook is today, as a major global presence." (Ries, 2011)

"More, more, more" isn't the automatic answer to business success. After all, Facebook started in a dorm room. Staying "lean" goes hand in hand with learning how to scale a business — and it all comes down to doing more with less. Keep costs down, only hire people for the jobs you need done, keep work moving, and constantly listen to your customers.

Recurring Revenue: Build a Business That Earns $10,000 Every Month

As a company, do you have the opportunity to benefit from owning a recurring revenue business model that will bring you a minimum amount of money each month through a subscription-based product or service? In this model, customers pay for a service on a consistent basis.

Cash flow can be a major dilemma for a lot of companies. You will have good and bad months, which makes budgeting and predicting income extremely hard. Subscriptions can make that see-saw experience easier to manage and predict.

Spotify's impact on the music industry is a great example of the power of recurring revenue. Those customers who use a paid version can cut out ads and listen to unlimited songs for a monthly fee, while a free version includes ads. This setup is not just for big companies; smaller companies can use it, too. Examples of industries that use recurring revenue include:

- **Wine houses:** Subscribe to be the first to receive new wines monthly or quarterly.

- **Local fitness studios:** Pay a monthly fee to join the club and take classes.

- **Data businesses:** Subscribe to monthly data packages to stay abreast of trends and issues.

Recurring revenue benefits your company in several ways:

1. **Predictable income:** If one person signs up for your service, the likelihood that they will still be there next month is huge.

2. **Scalable income:** You can stop trading your time for one-off projects, but you are scaling.

3. **More time to improve your business:** You have more time to upgrade your services, which translates to more income and more time to enjoy the things you love to do.

Goal: Maximize Your Conversion Rates

Maximizing your conversion rate is your ultimate goal when making your processes scalable.

Your conversion rate represents the percentage of website visitors who take action on an offer by buying that product/service and becoming actual customers. It's a way to track the effectiveness of your messaging, as well as the numbers of product/service sold behind the message. For more on conversion rates, see Figure 4.2: FunnelIQ.

Example: In the month of April, 100,000 people visit an e-commerce site. During that month, 2,000 users purchase something from the site. Thus, the site's conversion rate (2,000/100,000) is 2%.

The broader your scope and the more marketing activities you use (webinar registrations, emails, landing-page signups, etc.), the more you can increase your conversion rate.

What's a good conversion rate? One that is higher than the average is now. In 2020, the average conversion rate for e-commerce websites is 2.86%. The average e-commerce website conversion rate in the U.S. stands at 2.63% compared to the global website conversion rate of 4.31%.[14]

Today's marketing and sales landscape looks vastly different from that of just a few decades ago. With the advent of the internet, blogging, social media, and a myriad of digital communications channels, the path to purchase is not a simple straight line, but a complex and varied web of twists and turns — and touchpoints.

---

14 https://www.invespcro.com/blog/the-average-website-conversion-rate-by-industry/.

Today's consumers are also increasingly immune to traditional advertising and sales methodologies, meaning they conduct more independent research and take more convincing before they're sold on making a purchase. That's why the buyer's journey may differ from one consumer to the next: They're not all listening to the same radio spots to learn about your company. They're not even being exposed to the same information about your brand from the same sources. Some may have discovered your company on the web, while others learned of your products or services through word-of-mouth recommendations. Some may read online reviews before engaging with your marketing team or filling out an online request for more information. Others will visit your website, read your blog, and evaluate your competition before engaging with your company.

What's more, when leads are passed from marketing to sales, they're expected to be "sales-ready," or at the decision-making stage in the buying journey. The myriad paths to purchase make it increasingly challenging to qualify leads effectively as sales-ready.

It takes 18 touches on average to generate a viable sales lead.[15] That means it takes multiple touches for a consumer to make the choice to request information — and even more for marketing to gather the information needed to determine whether a lead is ready to be passed to sales. At the early stages in the buyer's journey, consumers are often merely gathering information and building awareness about your products and services. Often, these interactions are not in-depth enough to provide the information necessary to qualify as leads.

---

15 https://www.saleshacker.com/average-touches-prospecting/.

Chapter Review

Take a moment now to check how scalable your systems are. Do you have the right systems in place to reach enough consumers? Do you automate these processes? Can you add recurring revenues to your operating systems? Use this chart to assess how ready your systems are so you can start scaling.

	Y	N
Most processes are supported by automated systems.		
We gain new customers through an effective lead-generation process.		
Our systems are prepared to scale (if we grow threefold, we have systems in place to handle it).		
We are listed in appropriate directories to generate more web traffic and reach our target audiences more efficiently.		
We have started blogging and have a regular schedule for posting.		
We go beyond blogging through activities such as videos on YouTube or Vimeo; hosting a podcast; infographics; conducting and releasing case studies; and hosting online courses, workshops, or webinars.		

RuLe 4

What Can't Be Measured Can't Be Improved: Success Panel

A recent study by HubSpot found that only 23% of companies are exceeding their revenue goals — and of those not exceeding their goals, 74% don't know the number of monthly visits, leads, marketing-qualified leads (MQLs), or sales opportunities they need.[16]

How can you grow your customer base and revenue streams when you don't know how leads are coming into or moving through your marketing funnel?

When you're tracking the right things, growth becomes much easier. Focus on metrics that make you a customer-centric organization so that you get actionable data and timely user feedback that pushes your company forward. Find out which marketing initiatives are creating value by improving results, boosting ROI, and delivering mature leads to your sales team. Being able to attribute revenue properly through each of your marketing activities is key to knowing where to place your resources to fuel growth.

---

16 https://blog.hubspot.com/marketing/miss-revenue-goals-chart

Basic metrics like lead volume and website traffic are important, but failing to dive deeper means you could be missing out on key insights into your marketing performance and valuable opportunities for improvement. Your MQL-to-SQL (sales-qualified lead) ratio, number of unengaged subscribers, and other advanced marketing metrics will give you deeper insight into what's driving your success and where you should focus your attention.

Don't just measure campaign results; measure the effort that goes into them as well. Evaluate campaign performance based on two factors: Did your efforts produce the desired outcomes? Did the outcome justify the resources required?

During my career at Lantmännen, I learned an important rule: Don't show all the data you have. One of the managers loved data and hired an expensive data analyst. After three months in business, we had a dashboard about new products, a dashboard about the top 10 sales products, a dashboard about this and that; seemingly hundreds of dashboards. Although each one on its own was great, the sheer volume made it nearly impossible to parse useful details from the set as a whole. I learned that metrics do matter, but only if they demonstrate the foundations of the business. Set a focus on what's important vs. what's nice to have. Limit your tracking points. An expert scaleur will only focus on one KPI at a time.

Track Your Team's Performance

Trying to do too much all at once is counterproductive. Many of us have a cluster of goals we want to achieve right now, but what ends up happening is achieving none of them. You go too narrow and so wide that nothing gets done. Nothing gets traction. Then you get frustrated and give up. Giving up is not the answer. Focusing on one thing is.

One of my favorite focus tools is the team dashboard from Scaleurs.com. Use it to scale your team by dedicating only one simple KPI per team member. This is the tool we use at CHD Expert: Every team member is responsible for reaching their personal goal each year, which is evaluated into a SMART goal weekly and monthly.

SMART goals must meet the following criteria and can be used to determine your KPI:

- *Simple*: People need to know it and remember it easily.

- *Measurable*: There must be an objective way to determine whether or to what extent you have achieved your goal.

- *Achievable*: Don't aim so high that the goal can't be reached or so low that employees are left with nothing to do.

- *Realistic/Relevant*: Every goal must relate to your function or service.

- *Timewise*: Deadlines should be short, realistic, and finite.

For example, the content writer's goal is to attract the interest of consumers. KPI: Write five valuable content pieces per week, 20 pieces per month, or 240 pieces of content per year. Breaking the yearly goal into a smaller chunk (five per week) will still yield an impressive 240 pieces at the end of the year — writing five pieces of content per week seems a lot more manageable than 240 pieces per year.

For the social media manager, the goal is to target the right companies and business profiles using what the content writer produces. KPI: Win five MQLs per week, 20 MQLs per month, or 240 MQLs per year.

The PPC manager ensures that people find the company on Google and visit the website by fulfilling their goal of improving the company's keyword ranking. The goal of the website builder is to erase all the friction a customer might encounter when spending time on the website (e.g., incessant pop-up ads, buttons that are not clickable, links that do not work, information that is hard to find, etc.) so that a customer can be converted into an MQL.

Wouldn't it be great if, as a company, you suddenly could gain 240 new customers in a year?

Do you follow the logic? Everyone might have a different KPI, but together, they are striving for the same overarching marketing goal: getting more qualified demos to reduce the customer acquisition cost. The content writer must write good content so the social media manager can target and capture the right leads.

This snapshot of the dashboard for Scaleurs.com could be helpful (see Figure 4.1: Scaleurs DashIQ).

Figure 4.1: Scaleurs DashIQ

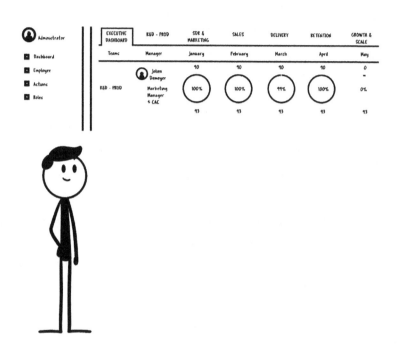

One of the challenges small companies might have is that the marketing department consists of only one team member or a small team. As discussed above, outsourcing is a good way to expand the talent pool.

At Marketing Scaleurs, the marketing team comprises three people. I used a great Danish company called Web 2 Media (W2M) to supplement our compact team. W2M has different sub-departments to deal with all the above functions and account managers who serve as your go-to. At Marketing

Scaleurs, I work with consultants from W2M's social media team, their pay per click team, and the analytics team. Together, they strongly supplement and contribute to our in-house team. Staying lean doesn't mean running your team (or yourself) into the ground. As your marketing business begins to scale, it can create an atmosphere of uneasiness and instability for everyone. Keep your top talent from looking elsewhere by holding regular check-ins and taking their feedback seriously. Recognize them for their hard work and celebrate the effort they're putting in to help your business grow. Scaling is an opportunity to give employees more responsibility, and even expose them to new parts of the business they haven't worked in before. Including them in product planning and projects like your strategic roadmap will help them discover new skills and prove that their input matters. They'll have a sense of ownership — and be there when your business fully transforms from small to scaled.

Lastly, a little bit of patience with your reps can go a long way. There is no magical "on" switch for scaling a marketing team. Just like adapting to a company is a learning experience for your new hires, scaling is a learning experience for budding businesses. Scaling doesn't happen overnight. Don't overextend yourself at the beginning of the process. Scaling a marketing team takes time.

9 Key Marketing Metrics

These metrics can be used for the dashboard tool from Scaleurs. com (see previous image). This will help you define and tailor the KPIs for your business.

1. Lead Volume: Lead-to-Customer Conversion Rate

Obviously, it's important to measure how many leads your marketing efforts are generating. But if you stop there, you're missing a crucial piece of the puzzle: how many leads actually turn into customers. Knowing this figure can tell you whether your sales team needs a higher volume of leads, higher-quality leads, or additional supporting content to help close deals.

How to measure it: The benchmark for conversion rates will vary by industry, but a few minutes of Googling should give you a solid understanding of the number you should be aiming to outperform. It's also important to consider conversion rates at each stage of the funnel: The middle and bottom of your funnel rates should be higher than your top-of-funnel numbers.

You can create your own funnel by using the FunnelIQ made by Marketing Scaleurs (see Figure 4.2: FunnelIQ) as one way to visualize each stage of the funnel, from first touch to lead conversion to opportunity creation, and gain a deeper understanding of the customer journey. Compare that number with the result you found with Google to see if you are on the right track.

Marketing is always seen as a cost, and few people know their ROMI (return on marketing investment). In times of crisis, marketing almost always is sacrificed first, even though that's when it's needed most.

To prevent losing out on invaluable marketing opportunities during a crisis, use the FunnelIQ from Marketing Scaleurs. How does it work? The first thing to ask when building a dashboard is what matters most. That is, what metrics are really going to move your business forward. Monitor the marketing KPIs that actually drive growth. Track your conversation rate throughout the funnel and over time.

The FunnelIQ consists of four parts:

1. ML (Marketing Leads): These leads consist of external traffic from search engines, social networks, paid media and IP addresses on your websites and blogs (i.e, the number of organic and paid visits to your website and blogs and the number of people following you on social media channels, which might come from your Google Analytics).

2. MQL (Marketing-Qualified Leads): These leads come people who have already given their permission to use their personal information. They arise from the number of actual clicks on an email address, phone number, or submission form. These figures come from tools like HubSpot or from those people who downloaded an infographic or requested an ebook on your social media platforms.

3. SL (Sales Leads): These leads are comprised of people who have actually scheduled demos. You can find these figures on your CRM system, like Salesforce.

4. SQL (Sales-Qualified Leads): These represent the number of quotes that are sent from your CRM system, like Salesforce or Microsoft Dynamics.

At the end of the funnel, you will see the conversion percentage and the number of sales won. That way, you can track it over time and see how your conversion rate is doing and if it is growing.

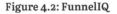

Figure 4.2: FunnelIQ

2. Point of Conversion: Multi-Touch Attribution

Very few people research and buy during the same web browsing session. Most people will start their search for a product or stumble across a piece of content, click through to your website, and poke around your blog, but not necessarily buy your service or product. Days or even weeks later, they will search for your company name, click on a paid ad, and purchase. By only crediting the point of conversion, you're not getting a full picture of the customer journey, and you're undervaluing key aspects of your marketing efforts.

How to measure it: You can use many types of attribution models, depending on what you want to learn and how your marketing organization works. Marketing Scaleur's FunnelIQ can be one way to give credit to each stage of the funnel, from first contact to lead conversion to opportunity development, and gain a deeper awareness of the customer journey. In this attribution model, 30% of the credit goes to the first click, 30% of the credit goes to the click that created the lead conversion, and 30% goes to the click that created the opportunity. 10% of the credit goes to all other touches.

For both Unibake and CHD, I set up a dashboard to use to set and reach monthly objectives. I look at the dashboard to see if there have been any big changes in the past month and where we should adapt accordingly. Together with W2M, we draft a plan for the next month and adjust along the way.

3. Blog Visitors: Engaged Time Spent

It's not enough to measure time spent on a page, because you don't know if it's active time or your content is just sitting open in an idle tab. Tracking engaged time lets you know how long users are actively paying attention to your content, and therefore how valuable that content is to your target audience. Are they even seeing your call to action (CTA)? What can you leave out that people aren't paying attention to, and what do you need to rework?

How to measure it: Content analytics software like Chartbeat or even WordPress plugins like Riveted can track user activity, including scrolling, clicking, using the keyboard, and page visibility, to determine whether the reader is actively engaging with your content or in an idle state.

If you have a blog, it is important to understand what people do and don't like about it. Which articles do they spend the most time on? You must deliver content that brings the most value to your customers.

4. Number and Quality of Inbound Links

High-quality websites are judged by search engines as trustworthy and reputable resources. Having low-quality websites linked to your website can even penalize your rankings, which is why it's much more important to have a few high-quality links rather than dozens of low-quality ones. Instead of tracking the number of inbound links you're getting, focus instead on these questions: How have certain inbound links helped you rank for certain keywords? Is your organic traffic increasing?

How to measure it: To determine quality links, check whether the site is relevant to your site, authoritative/trustworthy, attracting a human audience or solely designed for web crawlers, or linking to other spammy sites (online gambling, payday loans, etc.).

The Zapier tool lets you collect all of your leads in an Excel file after each campaign. It shows you the leads based on company name, job title, or other form fields (depending on your input) if leads are qualified based on your criteria. Sales development reps (SDRs) can then call on these leads daily because they are "warmer" leads.

5. Social Media Reach/Engagement

While it's good to have a large number of followers of your social media platforms, it doesn't help your business if they aren't actually engaging with you. How many people are actually clicking on, responding to, and interacting with your posts? And who are they? Answering these questions will help ensure you're delivering the right content to the right people in the right places.

How to measure it: Engagement types vary depending on the social media platform. Keep an eye on Facebook's engagement score and number of clicks, likes, shares, and comments; Twitter retweets, replies, and favorites; Pinterest likes, comments, or re-pins; Google+ likes, comments, and shares, etc.

In general, I don't waste a lot of time on organic postings. I post once or twice daily to keep current customers engaged. What matters is the engagement by consumers on paid media. How is one campaign performing vs. the budget? How many people have completed an online form or request for information? These are much better indicators of a good lead.

For example, your business might receive a lead through a form at your website. By tracking its history, you could see that this person had previously engaged with a paid post two times but hadn't submitted the actual form. Two weeks later, the person visited the website again and filled in a form, so one of your sales team could contact them and close the deal.

6. Email Unsubscribes/Unengaged Subscribers

Some people who subscribe to your list won't stay engaged with your emails, which is why so many marketers keep an eye on how many recipients unsubscribe. But not everyone will go through the process of unsubscribing, especially when it takes fewer clicks to just trash emails that aren't of interest. For the health of your subscriber list, it's important to track unengaged subscribers.

How to measure it: Decide on your marketing department's definition of unengaged. Is it someone who hasn't clicked on an email in three months? A year? Then, consider implementing an automatic unsubscribe that will remove these recipients from your list, and send an email notifying them that they've been unsubscribed. Keep in mind that some email services route "graymail" messages with low engagement to the junk folder.

At CHD, we had a lot of contacts in our system. During our first email campaign, we noticed that around 50 people unsubscribed immediately. The good thing about using a tool like HubSpot is that you can see who unsubscribed. Sometimes it's better that less relevant leads get removed so you can spend time and effort on resources elsewhere.

7. Website Traffic: Conversion Rate

A lot of your marketing efforts go into driving traffic to your website, so of course you want to keep an eye on how many people you're successfully attracting to your site and where they're coming from — but if you only focus on visits without putting equal emphasis on conversion, you're wasting your time and money. Plus, putting a little effort into bumping up conversion rates can have a big impact on your business: Imagine the difference that even a 1 or 2% boost in new customers could do for your bottom line.

How to measure it: First, define what qualifies as a conversion. Is it a purchase? Booking a consultation or requesting additional information? Signing up for a free trial? Once you've figured out exactly what you want to measure, set up a landing page that visitors will only see after they've converted. Just make sure traffic can't be sent to that page in any other way, or else you'll get skewed figures.

Before starting, make sure your tracking pixels are installed. Google Tag Manager, Google Analytics, Google Console, and Social Media Pixels are critical for measuring web traffic for website conversion rates. If you get a lead, you want to know where it came from.

8. Number of MQLs: MQL-to-SQL Ratio

Marketing-qualified leads (MQLs) are generally defined as bottom-of-the-funnel prospects who have indicated they're ready to purchase, or at least talk to a salesperson, by downloading buying guides, requesting a demo, or signing up for a free trial. Sales-qualified leads (SQLs) are those potential customers who sales determines are ready for a direct follow-up. Looking at the percentage of MQLs that are accepted as SQLs is a good indicator of the health of your pipeline and your marketing team's ability to qualify and screen leads. It's also a great indication of how well your marketing and sales team are aligned and communicating with each other, since a low ratio raises a red flag that there's a disconnect between marketing and sales.

How to measure it: Divide the number of SQLs by the number of MQLs to calculate your MQL-to-SQL conversion rate. What's a good benchmark? After analyzing hundreds of companies, Implicit found that the average conversion rate was 13% and that it took an average of 84 days to convert.[17] But keep in mind: That number varies greatly depending on the source of the lead. For example, website leads converted at an average of 31.3%, referrals

---

17 https://www.salesforce.com/blog/2014/11/b2b-sales-benchmark-research-finds-some-pipeline-surprises-infographic-gp.html.

at 24.7%, and webinars at 17.8%, while email campaigns convert at just 0.9%, lead lists at 2.5%, and events at 4.2%. Check monthly to track the cost of acquisition and see if you have the right leads in-house.

9. External/Internal Metrics

Obviously, it's important to keep an eye on external metrics like lead quantity, quality, and conversion. But if (when) any of these numbers start to slip, how will you know what you need to fix if you don't pay attention to how the work gets done in the first place? When it comes to getting the most out of your internal resources, don't just trust your gut. Keep your marketing team running effectively by tracking the number of hours wasted in status meetings, repeatable work that could be automated, and dealing with unnecessary interruptions, as well as the efficiency of your review and approvals process.

How to measure it: Hold frequent check-ins with your team to identify roadblocks and gather feedback about how processes can be improved.

Grow by the Data — Avoid Spending on Speculation

The key to sustainable growth is in your hard data. These can come from a variety of sources and often revolve around your customers and prospects, including:

- How customers move through your sales funnel
- How long it takes to convert
- How long they remain a customer
- What causes them to leave/stay
- How they engage with you

- What attracts their attention

- Their pain points

- The biggest complaints or issues with your product/service

- What they love about your business

While it's important to spend money on things that help with operations and fulfillment to ensure your company can handle growth, you should also spend money on data-driven marketing. This includes both marketing to acquire new customers and marketing to engage existing ones.

Yes, you need money to fuel growth, but if your primary strategy is pure spending, you're setting yourself up to fail. Once your team is used to a culture of spending, it's extremely hard to roll back and put accountability into place. Learn from the tech companies that went bankrupt in the late 1990s when the capital markets dried up. Instead be laser-focused on your investments, especially when it comes to marketing: Bet on content marketing, not ads, and use the proper tools to ensure you're making data-driven decisions.

When you pay attention to the data, you'll be able to address major issues, like the causes of customer churn or leaks in your sales funnel that are limiting acquisitions. Your site analytics, survey responses, social insights, and customer data can reveal a wealth of opportunities where taking action will have a significant impact on the growth and scalability of your organization.

Chapter Review

Now that you have a good sense of the factors involved with metrics and data, here are some aspects to assess. Remember, the company should have an overall growth rate goal, and that goal should be split it up per department and per person (see Figure 4.3: Company Growth Rate).

	Y	N
We know our company growth rate.		
Our objectives have been translated into clear, measurable indicators.		
We have real-time data that report how we are progressing toward reaching our goals.		
Each department knows its goals.		
Each team member knows their goals.		

Figure 4.3: Company Growth Rate

Revenue two years ago	2.3	million	your growth
Revenue last year	2.6	million	13%
Revenue target this year	2.9	million	12%

What are you company's growth objectives?

(In comparison to last year's sales in millions of USD, for example 15.4)

Revenue next year	3.5	million	21%
Revenue target in two years	4	million	14%

BONUS RULE 5

Keep It Simple and Have Fun

When you scale operations, it can be tempting to go nuts with the processes you bring in. It's an exciting and scary time for any business, and there are so many strategies out there that you can adopt. But it's also a time to stop and take a step back.

The easiest way to maintain consistency in your business processes is to keep them simple, especially during a time of change and flux. Successful business leaders are often so because they learn how to simplify things. They take the complex and make it less so. This approach to business is used in everything from launching products to developing workflows.

Complexity sucks up time. It requires more meetings, more explanations, more-refined communication with the customer, more people in the workflow, and more cogs in the machine. Complexity slows businesses down and inhibits growth. As a business grows and scales, the key dynamic that slows progress is the effect of complexity. CEOs who are most effective in reducing complexity tend to have a clear and well-communicated vision of the company's goals, an ability to lead employees toward that vision, and a willingness to change course when it becomes clear that certain strategies are not providing the required results.

Keeping your processes simple also makes it easy to stay engaged with the people who are the greatest component of your growth and success: your customers. When you focus on one thing (or just a few things), your marketing business will remain simple, too.

No Shortcuts in Scaling

As your business begins to grow, you may be tempted to make cuts — and take shortcuts — to reach your next goal faster, but there's no more surefire way to cripple your business than to cut corners and try to take the easy path to success.

Every action you take now has repercussions later. Focusing too heavily on your end goal of scaling your business can impede the attainment of interceding goals that lead up to it. The problem with making an extrinsic reward the only destination that matters is that some people will choose the quickest route there, even if it means taking the low road.

When you take shortcuts, you make compromises. You compromise your ethics, values, and the integrity of your business — often at the expense of the customer and your employees. Dallas Mavericks owner and Shark Tank host Mark Cuban remembers the best advice about success in business that he ever received: "Do the work. Out-work. Out-think. Out-sell your expectations. There are no shortcuts."[18]

Keeping it simple works for your website and making sure it's lead-conversion friendly. Instead of giving visitors a single page with more than a dozen CTAs, rethink that arrival experience. How can a customer start navigating and find what they want

---

18 https://www.businessinsider.com/mark-cuban-reveals-best-and-worst-shark-tank-pitches-2013-11.

when inundated with so much superfluous information? A website that is hastily put together and ill-designed will chase customers away rather than welcome them in. Don't cut corners when you talk about foundations. If necessary, start over — but without taking shortcuts. To create a website that will help your business scale, you might have to restart from scratch with a new design and a great engineer who really knows their stuff. The result will be worth the effort.

Survival Tips for When Your Business Is Scaling Too Quickly

Every company experiences growing pains — they're a normal and necessary part of the journey of building a company — but don't be fooled into thinking that too many orders or too many clients are "good" problems to have. On the contrary, scaling your business too fast can quickly ruin your entire brand. That's why you have do the best-quality work at all times. After all, it's much easier to do things right from the beginning than to repair a broken reputation.

Take this example: An online clothing company grew incredibly fast. After running a marketing campaign, sales skyrocketed, and the company had to increase their manufacturing from 2,000 units to 45,000 in a single week. They ran into problems with fulfillment almost immediately, and customers began complaining that they weren't delivering on time.

What was the underlining reason? They never considered whether the whole organization was set up to scale, and they never communicated internally that they would be investing in such a campaign. If the number of inbound leads increases, sales have to follow — and so does delivery/fulfillment.

You can already imagine the customer complaints, cancellations, and damage done to their brand.

The good news? They responded *immediately*. They talked with their design and marketing agency, and opted for a campaign that communicated a vital message: We screwed up, we know, help is coming, and we will give you a bonus for the next time. By doing that, they improved customer retention; most of their customers bought again from the revamped, improved website. It's okay to make mistakes, and there are ways to recover, but avoiding these mistakes is the better option.

How to Avoid Scaling Too Quickly

What I learned from all my experiences is that when scaling your business, you need a plan for growth if you want to survive. The following tips reinforce the lessons we've learned over the course of the book. These are time-tested techniques to keep your business afloat when you're in over your head.

These are my 4 S's of scaling:

1. **Strategy.** Make an annual timeline. It's vital to have a roadmap for where you want to go, how to get there, and when you want to arrive. Your annual plan can include how many clients or customers you want to have by the end of the year, as well as what kind of time commitment is required once there are 10, 20, or more. Your timeline should also include your goals for partners, employees, and sales funnels. The more you plan for, the better your chance of success.

2. **Success Panel**. Monitor your timeline. Once you have a plan in place, you should implement some kind of system to keep track of your progress and how much time you spend on each client. If you can't meet your timeline, or you get an influx of new clients all of a sudden, you have to figure out how to change your plan so you can still do a good job. This may require you to temporarily pay an agency or consulting company to help you until you put a better system in place. The dashboard of Scaleurs.com will also help you to define and track your timeline. Think about where you are now vs. where you want to go and why. Use that to define a SMART KPI, and that KPI is what you will track in your team or executive dashboard from Scaleurs.

3. **Scaleur's Mindset**. Be open to change and scaling up. Make sure you don't have too much on your plate. If someone on your team feels overwhelmed, you have no choice but to help them. If you feel overwhelmed, you need a way to step back and assess so you can cope. Building a cohesive team means that everybody gets involved, and everyone owns a certain part of a project, so be proactive by asking your team how they're doing and advocating for your people by seeing who can help pitch in to assist them. If there's too much on your employee's plate, you can hire outside help, ask someone else to contribute, or just do it yourself. Hiring outside help and asking others to step up can take some of the load off you.

Find people to outsource tasks to. It can be tempting to want to do everything yourself, but you don't have enough time, energy, or know-how to do all that's required to run your company. Know when it's time to outsource, delegate, and get things off your plate. Rather than waste time on bolstering your weaknesses, focus your efforts on your strengths and the big picture of growing your company.

Find strategic partners; they make life easier for you, whether they provide you with data, exchange clients with you, or refer clients to your company. Say you don't make websites, but your strategic partner does. You can include them on projects that require building a site for your client (or even improving your own site), and they can refer clients to you — it's a win-win. Mutually beneficial relationships help grow your business and allow you to focus more of your time on your core competency.

Build a deliberate environment. There's a balance between making sure that your employees are happy and performing at a high level. A big part of building company morale is making sure every choice you make — whether it's vacation policy, chain of command issues, or workflow processes — is clearly communicated and well understood. Being a team member is a job in and of itself, so share in the stress and in the reward.

4. **Systems.** Have the right systems and processes in place. Remember, it's more important to deliver on time than to pull in more clients. Most startups fail because of bad management. When you have lots of clients, you have to prioritize. Your first step is to deliver high-

quality work on time, which is more important than landing additional leads or clients, so devise a plan for scaling in a smart, effective way. Make a budget, come up with a forecast, and prepare for how you're going to grow while also maintaining quality.

Good communication solves almost any problem. As a marketing leader, the ability to communicate with your employees and your partners about an upcoming uptick in workload will help address anyone's feelings of being overwhelmed. If your team feels inundated with work, you have to motivate them and offer to help or outsource tasks.

Don't be afraid to move on. Some companies spend a huge amount of time and money on trying to please difficult clients. But there are millions of companies in the U.S. alone to work with, so there's no need for your business to stand or fall on one client, or waste energy and resources on ones that are unpleasant, overly demanding, slow in paying, or otherwise problematic. If the terms aren't working for you, negotiate them or drop the client.

Remember that failing to plan is planning to fail. If you scale smart, you can deliver the best work to your clients while also growing as a company by scaling.

Enjoy the Ride

The arduous process of scaling might seem like it can't be fun, and there is a common notion that scaleurs are fun-averse workaholics who spend all their time building their brands and scaling up their businesses or marketing efforts, but smart scaleurs understand that time should be set aside for fun and recreation. It should not be about work all the time. I have been a scaleur for quite a while, and I have had to learn from other smart scaleurs that work should not be the sole focus of your days. As a matter of fact, one of the world's most successful entrepreneurs, Richard Branson, has said, "If you are spending most of your life at work, it should not be a chore, and it should be fun!"

Here are a few things that I believe will make you a fun-loving, unstressed, and productive scaleur.

1. **Make your work *part* of your life, not your life itself.**

Building a business is never easy. As an owner or entrepreneur there's always more you can do, and there are demands on your time 24/7. It is important that as a scaleur, you understand that you work to live — you do not live for work alone. Your work is part of your life, not your life. Find a way to separate your work life from your personal life. Make a conscious effort to keep doing this until it's internalized.

I've always tried to leave time for simple pleasures, such as taking an hour to go for a run or being with friends on the weekends, no matter where work-related travel takes me. The startup world moves at lightning speed, but even so, it's important to use the time that helps you recharge and think. I have some of my best ideas while exercising or relaxing on vacation. Finding balance leads you to the right answers at work, too.

Don't forget that vacations are a great avenue for re-invigoration, re-strategizing, and creativity. A change from your usual work environment gives you the opportunity to achieve a little distance and objectivity; to see things differently and better. Consider combining business trips with leisure trips; meet new people, and learn about their culture.

2. **Cultivate a unique culture.** The culture you nurture from day one is a huge part of your company's success. Organizations need to foster their culture organically because at the end of the day, it's about people. Creating an outstanding work culture that accurately represents a company's values begins with strong leadership. When leadership creates and embodies a work culture that matches the company's mission and vision, it becomes part of the company DNA. In today's workplace, company culture is a major factor in attracting and retaining employees, and a lot of companies are working to create an engaging work environment that stands out against the more traditional workplaces and appeals to newer generations.

As an example, at Unibake, a small group of us created a work group named "Shiny Happy People." Our goal was to do little things for our employees, because these little things matter the most. These included:

- Hosting a yearly "country battle," a friendly competition aimed at team-building that was also a way for employees to represent their home countries.

- Celebrations when we launched a new product.

- Painting the company values on the walls of meeting rooms.

- Volunteer work.

- Doing "fika" sessions (Swedish for having a coffee with a pastry while chatting with colleagues for 15 minutes).

3. **Embrace open communication.** If you are going to lead a successful business, you must create an environment with open communication and trust. Open communication allows your employees to be more engaged and understand that what they do matters in the success of the business. Making sure your employees understand the big picture and the part they play in the success of the organization will help them understand why decisions are made and how those decisions affect them specifically and the company as a whole. Effective communication will get everyone on the same page and moving in the same direction toward the same goal.

Effective communication seems simple, but it does take effort. Management should communicate their goals as well as those of the company. Routinely talking with your employees about their goals, both personal and professional, will create accountability for both management and employees. When an issue surfaces, it must be dealt with immediately so everyone can move on. You have to walk the walk if you truly want managers and employees to share ideas and opinions.

When looking to introduce a more fun-oriented workplace, be careful in how you do it. Certain measures should be avoided. *Don't carry out survey-type testing* of the cultural temperature if it's the only time you collect feedback on "fun" at work. *Don't install leisure activities* like ping-pong or video games from the top down because that can come across as "enforced fun." And *don't turn fun into a target* that has to be reached. Foster its growth; don't force its death.

Somewhere along the way, many entrepreneurs forget to have fun when scaling their businesses. After a while, you might get bogged down with details or you might get burned out. Mitigate your scaleur workaholism with enjoyment of the process. You'll appreciate reaching the destination more if you can savor the journey along the way.

PART THREE

The Scaleur's Toolkit

One of the biggest misunderstandings about scaling marketing efforts is that it requires you to do *more marketing*. It's not about *more* marketing; it's about more effectively using your marketing tools. This chapter provides an overview of what your toolkit should look like based on what we discussed in the previous chapters. Select and use the marketing tools that offer the biggest return for the least cost and effort.

In most situations, a combination of email and social media marketing is the most cost-effective way to reach the maximum number of people in your target audience. The trick is to engage the 20% of your customers who will drive 80% of your business. Then, expand your reach by investing time in the one or two social networks where the majority of your customers are most active. This strategy will drive repeat business and amplify the reach of your messages through social sharing and word of mouth.

Lead-Generation Tools

Building a predictable lead-generation machine to support scaling a business is challenging. Once you crack this challenge, though, it's extremely rewarding because it helps you scale up faster and afford to be more selective with whom you work with. In the B2B world, most customer relationships today begin with content offers, then continue with lead nurturing through the sales funnel. You must understand the full nurturing model and have various types of content (from ebooks to webinars) to serve specific audience needs throughout your funnel. These tools will help you get there.

- *Leadfeeder*: A website visitor tracking tool that tells you which businesses are visiting your website, even if the visitor does not fill out a form or download a resource. Using a website visitor tracking tool (which is similar to analytics, but with the ability to identify which individual companies visit your website) is an effective method of lead capture. By identifying the businesses visiting your site and monitoring the pages they visit and the content they read, you can develop outreach and engagement opportunities based on their actual site engagement.

- *Product Hunt*: A go-to launch platform for startups and enterprises that are putting new products in the market. It has a pre-existing community of testers and early adopters who are willing to try new products.

- *Sumo*: A multi-app toolkit built to increase the ROI of your website. It offers a variety of pop-up tools designed to drive lead captures on every page of your website, including newsletter sign-up, special offers, and lower cart-abandonment rates through timely pop-up reminders during checkout. Sumo integrates with most email service providers to ensure your leads go straight to your lists. Alternatives are Sleeknote and Hello Bar.

- Fomo: A way to leverage the power of social proof to increase conversions. While customers and prospects are browsing your website, Fomo displays small notifications alerting your prospects about other visitors on the site, as well as some of the purchases those other visitors have made. By showing prospects what other customers are viewing and purchasing, you instantly give your website and business credibility through social proof.

- Snip.ly: Adds a call to action on every link you share. Even if you are sharing a non-branded website, Snip.ly lets you display a branded call to action on those sites, meaning you can engage customers and prospects with every piece of content you share with them.

- Drift: A way to capture more qualified leads based on who visits your site. Drift creates conversational bots that interact with your website visitors. By setting predetermined questions and answers to commonly asked questions and tailoring these questions to different pages on your site, you can help potential new leads find the information they're looking for quickly and boost conversation on lead-generation pages. This tool also gives you the ability to connect with your support team directly for any interactions that require a more "human" touch.

Analytics Tools

Data visualizers help reformat valuable, insightful data into visual graphs, charts, and graphics that make those numbers easier to digest. You have to know your numbers — if you don't know how much it costs you to generate leads and sales, down to the penny, you will crash and burn.

- *Google Analytics*: To keep a pulse on how users are interacting with your pages and products, take the time to set up Google Analytics on your e-commerce website. You'll be able to track sessions, users, pageviews, conversion events, time on page, bounce rates, and more. You can also set up reports that help identify problems or opportunities in real time.

- *FunnelIQ from Marketing Scaleurs*: Identify the leading indicators for the health of your marketing team and share progress in real time. Break down your marketing budget and understand your Return on Marketing Investment (ROMI). Become a data-driven marketer, make better decisions and improve performance, faster and easier, with DashIQ.

- *DashIQ from Scaleurs.com*: Triple your personal and business goals using a simple dashboard. The Scaleur Suite is composed of three applications. Each one consists of a visual dashboard allowing you to set specific goals, remain focused on what matters the most and track your exponential progress.

- *Segment*: Collect data points from every platform, aggregate into Segment, and then send that data to hundreds of tools for marketing, analytics, and data warehousing. With more than 200 source and destination integrations, Segment makes it possible for your business to coordinate and draw insights across multiple business units and teams. Alternatives are Urban Airship, Keen, Snowplow, and Mapp.

- MixPanel: A granular-data collection tool that allows you to analyze each customer interaction across the entire user journey. MixPanel captures each user interaction, so you can start to build touchpoints and customer journeys based on actual customer interaction history, leading to more-personalized customer experience and increased conversion rates. Alternatives include Amplitude, Woopra, and Localytics.

- Bitly: Create short links that track every click, tap, or swipe as users make their way across the internet. Branded links allow you to make sure campaign links have brand consistency. You can integrate Bitly with most social media and campaign management tools to ensure all of your messaging is tracked effectively.

- SharedCount: A simple application that lets you see where your site's URLs have been shared online, this program calculates the number of shares for a given URL in Facebook, Pinterest, and StumbleUpon.

- Autopilot: Capture new leads from your website, app, or blog and then nurture them with personalized messages. You can also use it to automate repetitive sales funnel tasks, such as lead assignation, appointment setting, and customer onboarding programs. Alternatives are Marketo and Pardot.

- Zapier: This automation tool lets you move data between your web applications so lead-generation flows and alert notifications can be automated seamlessly between your marketing tools.

- *Clearbit*: Tracking sales interactions and lead generation is important as you start to scale up your business, and Clearbit's Salesforce integration will automatically update any interactions with your leads based on a number of different sources. This tool will also help track leads through the entire sales funnel, helping you know exactly when to retarget or reach out and close the deal.

Content and Email Marketing Tools

Email marketing isn't new. As long as you're using it correctly, email is still one of the most valuable and most targeted channels for reaching your audience. These tools will help you understand open rates, A/B testing, and email lead nurturing.

- *Medium*: A popular blogging platform and an effective tool for generating valuable inbound content and growing a community. Most importantly, you can have your own hosted blog.

- *HubSpot*: A way to manage your leads pipeline. HubSpot also integrates with most lead-generation and email marketing platforms, so your lead generation efforts can be amplified through serious automation and easy-to-take actions. HubSpot's free CRM platform is also the foundation for their Marketing, Sales, and Service hub product sets, providing an end-to-end platform for lead generation, sales funnel management, and retention.

- *Mailchimp*: An email marketing and automation platform that allows you to grow and manage your newsletter and product subscribers.

- *Verify Email*: A simple service that verifies your email marketing lists. It connects to the email server and checks whether an email address exists or not, which is useful if you are re-engaging old leads or contacts.

- *Good Email Copy*: Provides a repository for time-tested, effective email copy for campaign inspiration. You can view email copy used for acquisition and onboarding campaigns from some of the most successful businesses in the world.

- *Campaign Monitor*: Sends personalized email campaigns to your customers so you can stay on top of your customer interactions. You can trigger messages to be sent based on a subscriber's location in the customer journey and increase conversion with relevant content. Use Campaign Monitor's robust analytics to create targeted segments of your email list and send emails with templates and content that inspire action.

Website SEO/PPC Tools

SEO is foundational to any marketing strategy, but it's tough to do effectively, especially in a crowded market, as everyone jostles to rank among the top search results and stay one step ahead of Google's periodically shifting algorithms. These tools can help you work around such headaches.

- *Unbounce*: Build high-conversion landing pages for campaigns and events. Using a simple drag-and-drop editor, you can easily build landing pages optimized for data capture and lead generation. You can also run A/B tests to test landing-page copy and layout to ensure your pages are always optimized for lead capture.

- *Optimize*: Part of the Google Marketing Platform, this is a comprehensive website testing tool that allows you to run tests on your website copy, layout, and calls to action so you can make sure your site runs at its best for each and every visitor. Optimize integrates natively with Google Analytics, so you can start to draw insights about your website immediately and run A/B, multivariate, and redirect tests to learn what works best for your site visitors.

- *Olark*: Providing live-chat applications for businesses, this tool offers a no-fuss approach to live-chat software that has improved its design over the past couple of years. Olark also offers an extensive integration portfolio to ensure chat leads captured on your site are sent to the right tools in your marketing stack.

- *Keyword Too*: Find complementary keywords using Google's autocomplete engine. Use this as an alternative to Google keyword research. The free version is capable of building 750+ long-tail keyword combinations. Alternatives are Google and Bing.

- *Semrush*: An all-in-one digital marketing tool and a comprehensive workflow tool for SEO, this platform allows you to audit your SEO performance, track positions for keywords, generate ideas for gaining traffic, and monitor competitors. Semrush also offers analytics for paid online campaigns and social media;

however, their strongest offering is their organic analytics component.

- *Google Ads:* To increase brand and product exposure, you can use Google Ads to create campaigns that drive more customers to your website. You can target specific audiences based on location or keywords, and you only pay for actual results. What makes Google Ads extra special is that you don't have to create the demand — you simply have to satisfy it, because your audience is already looking for your products and using your keywords.

Design Tools

Posts that contain images and videos increase engagement because of the visual and aesthetic appeal. With these tools, you don't have to be a design expert to make them work.

- *Visme:* A simple online interface to generate images to accompany marketing campaigns. Whether you're creating images for social media, printed brochures, websites, product mockups, business cards, or online display ads, anyone can use Visme use for marketing images. Alternatives are Canva, Gimp, Photoshop, and InDesign.

- *Photoshop:* You can use Photoshop to create professional-grade product images to insert throughout your website. Customize and edit photos and graphics to establish a sense of consistency and branding that will differentiate you from competitors. Professional photo editing can also help build trust and legitimacy for your e-commerce business.

- *Lumen5*: Create engaging video ads and start publishing high-quality video content to social media. With a stock image gallery and more than 2,000 video templates, Lumen5 gives you the ability to create professional-looking videos through their drag-and-drop builder. You can also perform multivariate tests to see which videos connect best with your audience.

Social Media Tools

Some of the most popular social media networks are Facebook, YouTube, Twitter, Instagram, LinkedIn, and Tumblr, which are used often in both paid and unpaid marketing. These specialized tools can enhance their value for your marketing efforts by helping you manage your various social media accounts from one spot.

- *Buffer*: Coordinated social media marketing is one of the most effective marketing tools available to companies of any size. Social media management platforms allow you to automate and batch the entire social media marketing process. Plan and curate your content calendar, compose and schedule your messages, and then spread them out over the course of a day or week. Alternatives are Hootsuite, Sprout Social, Crowdfire, and MeetEdgar.

- *Livestorm*: This webinar platform is GDPR[19]-ready and delivers a HIPPA[20]-compliant streaming technology as well.

---

19 GDPR: General Data Protection Regulation

20 HIPPA: Health Insurance Portability and Accountability Act

- *Facebook Ads*: To connect with new customers and drive them to your e-commerce site, use Facebook Ads to launch campaigns that target specific users or types of users. This is a great option for e-commerce businesses because it is relatively inexpensive compared to other options. My favorite part of using Facebook Ads is that you can get incredibly specific when it comes to targeting your ideal customer.

- *Criteo*: To create more-compelling ads for visitors, use Criteo to create and launch personalized retargeting ad campaigns. With Criteo, you can convert more shoppers by presenting them with dynamic ads that recommend the best offers and products from your catalog. The tool also allows you to optimize campaign performance by automatically selecting creative components that are likely to drive the most engagement.

- *AdEspresso*: To optimize your Facebook Ads, use AdEspresso to create simple A/B tests to determine which ads perform better. With robust analytics, you can easily see how well your campaigns are faring. This tool will also provide suggestions for the best way to optimize your campaigns according to various metrics.

Productivity Tools

Managing your business often gets in the way of growing your business — and it just gets more annoying the larger you grow. These tools can help you manage your time, finances, people, and channels, and even conduct competitive analysis so you can stay ahead of the game.

- *Hiver, Basecamp, Trello*: As your team grows, communication becomes vastly more important. With tools like these, you can maintain a cleaner, more streamlined inbox by removing cc, bcc, and forwarding entirely. Shared mailboxes give your team the ability to assign tasks to one another and remove any difficulties that come along with multiple team members interacting with customers through the same email address.

- *ShipStation*: This program lets you streamline, automate, and scale fulfillment and shipping for your business. You can also use it to import, manage, and ship product orders. ShipStation integrates with a number of e-commerce shopping carts, platforms, and tools, including Sellbrite.

- *Jelloow.com*: Use this platform to grow your audience, find new customers, build your lead list, and turn them into loyal fans. Jelloow will guide your company to the right marketing agency that fits your needs. Compare each agency, then hire the one that's right for you.

Keeping pace with all these new touchpoints and tactics is challenging for even the most experienced marketer. That's why building out your marketing tech stack in a strategic and scalable way is so important. With adaptable, scalable marketing tools working behind the scenes, all kinds of opportunities will open up, and you'll have everything you need to stay one step ahead of the competition.

PART FOUR

Time to Scale the Right Way

Any business is undergoing a constant process of evolution and reinvention, and the business you're operating today will become radically different as it scales. The process involves a lot of trial and error. Embrace what serves you, and let go of what doesn't work. In some cases, be willing to throw out bad ideas completely.

If your business is ready and prepared to accommodate growth through scaling, then it is much more likely to survive, and it will have the durability and longevity to remain on the path to success.

A scalable business has numerous benefits:

- *Improved efficiency*: Scalable businesses are more efficient because they plan for all eventualities and ensure they can operate in different circumstances.

- *Consistency*: Businesses that scale effectively are better at delivering expected results reliably, no matter what problems emerge.

- *Adaptability*: Maintaining the flexibility to adapt to economic changes and pressures means knowing when to up-scale or down-scale as required.

- Longevity: Businesses that can carefully consider scalability are much more likely to survive far into the future.

- Competition: It should go without saying that if you have a scalable business and are successful as a result, you are a strong competitor in your field.

For businesses, the path to success is not in simply growing but in scaling your business. To effectively scale your marketing in particular and your business in general, you must be achieving exponential growth while keeping your costs fairly low. But truth be told, scaling a marketing business requires a whole new level of skills and systems that many entrepreneurs can't fully anticipate.

As you begin scaling your marketing and your business, you may find yourself experiencing increased expenses, customer support issues, and miscommunication between staff members. An existing bad process will only be amplified once you begin trying to scale.

Scale or Fail

Scaling isn't just about increasing or expanding. At some points, you also might have to scale down to meet lower demands or cope with unexpected growth. This could be a result of natural peaks and troughs in your business cycle, or a consequence of a recession or a fundamental change in your industry that is beyond your control. Either way, lots of factors can make or break a business, so it's important to be ready for whatever comes your way. Scalability is about knowing when to change tack and having the resources to do so. If you don't prepare to scale, then you can pretty much prepare to fail. Failures will inevitably occur as you scale. The secret ingredient that keeps failures from turning into disasters is the capacity to use mistakes to your advantage by *learning* from them and *adapting* — the old saw about "failing forward."

When your business is thriving and growing rapidly, ensure you have provisions to meet new demands. This might mean having access to a greater volume of products or the ability to increase staffing levels quickly to deliver a service. It may also mean having a cash flow plan that is sustainable and funds that can be moved about quickly. If there is a downturn or a sudden fall in demand, do you have a plan in place to cut costs and streamline the business so it can still run efficiently under pressure?

Ultimately, your business plan should take into consideration the changes that put pressure on scalability. This should be the key driver for your plan. If there is a limit to the production you can churn out, there is little point in executing a marketing strategy that is going to give you more sales than you can handle. Success is about finding the right balance to ensure your business can adjust to the ups and the downs, and knowing when to take your foot off the gas or ease up to comfortably meet changing demands.

Keep up with the changing world. Change is happening faster and faster, and the only way to thrive is to accept the inevitability of change. Move faster than your competition and race to the future. Build that business, instead of just creating a job.

Moreover, never forget that the starting point for scaling lies not in your capital, resources, infrastructure, clientele, or workforce, but within you: the scaleur's mindset. That means having the energy and desire to scale, and possessing a growth mindset that embraces change and uncertainty, thrives on challenges, and learns from failures.

If you've cultivated the right mentality for scaling, you are ready to ascertain whether your existing processes can be scaled. Existing processes will be under heavy strain as your output increases exponentially — can you align and standardize them to accommodate an explosive period of growth?

In almost all cases, this will require automation, which is largely a function of the right tools and technology. But processes also depend on *people* — and scaling, as with almost any function in business, demands that you have the right team in place. In a broad sense, this means having a team that lives and breathes the company values and gels with the company culture. You need the right mix of generalists and specialists to cover all the bases. Areas that in-house staff can't cover must be filled in by outside help (freelancers, contract labor, outsourcing, etc.), or you're going to have a rocky time with managing a corporate growth spurt.

Remember the nine core marketing positions that comprise your "A-team." In smaller organizations, the same people may play more than one role, but fulfilling all of them is a key step toward successful scaling.

Meanwhile, you must emphasize your differentiators as a company. Scaling is not achieved from wishful thinking or sheer will — if you wish to scale up, you must have something *original, compelling, and marketable* to entice a vastly expanded clientele. A differentiator fulfills three criteria: It must be true; it must be valuable to potential clients; and it must be provable.

This principle goes hand in hand with delighting your customers. If you haven't figured out how to delight a thousand, how will you delight a million? Delighting your customers in a business that scales means delivering exponentially greater rewards to your target market without a corresponding exponential increase in resource expenditures. That means doing what you've always done well while finding new ways to bring that delight to a larger audience. If you find yourself struggling with this rule as you scale, go back to the basics: A big part of customer delight involves personalization and communication, which, by their nature, are easier to do on a smaller scale. Don't lose that individual, human touch when you go big. It's not just a sentimental notion; it's a prerequisite to scaling.

If content is the currency of marketing, repurposing that content is like investing currency in a booming bull market — you reap a sizable return on your investment without having to create it anew. Repurpose, don't repeat, your existing content. The internet provides a panoply of digital media and channels where you can adapt content you already have, which is conducive to scaling. In this way, you can easily maximize your online presence. Input your existing content into a matrix — your rows are the content, and the columns are the chosen medium for that content (podcasts, webinars, blogging, vlogging, etc.). You need 8 to 10 touchpoints to convert a customer, so your content engine has to be firing on all cylinders if you are to grow efficiently.

As the process of scaling unfolds, make sure you measure progress using the key marketing metrics discussed earlier.

Finally, have fun with it. It will at times be stressful, strenuous, and tear-your-hair-out frustrating. Embrace these difficulties as an unavoidable part of the challenge. They'll make the victories that much sweeter — and there will be victories. If you follow the rules I've laid out, little by little, you'll see that scaling actually *works*. Even though you hoped and expected it would, it will still feel like a little miracle taking shape, something marvelous to behold, when you see the results. Don't forget to enjoy these moments as your vision emerges into a fully functional, smoothly running *machine*, for that is really what a business that has successfully scaled is: a marvel of people, process, and technology working in tandem; a system unto itself.

I've been involved in startups, large corporate conglomerates, smaller specialized firms, and now my own marketing consultancy, so when it comes to marketing and scaling, I've seen it all. Now, as I build my own company, I embrace the process with a heady mix of exhilaration and (I admit) nervousness. Although I'm confident in the prospects of my business, entrepreneurship is always a major undertaking fraught with risk — there's so much at stake.

It took me three months to get my first lead. In the beginning, I didn't have a lot of capital to invest in marketing or in the business in general. As is often the case for startups, it was a very DIY approach, since I wasn't able to hire a staff or enlist outside professionals. Meanwhile, I was writing the first draft of this book, which was fortuitous because it helped me channel everything I'd learned over my career into my business. As the book developed, it became a guidebook for me to use to grow my own business.

Combined with blog writing, the right SEO, and a steady output of social media posts, I started to gain traction, based on the notion that if you offer valuable information for free, prospective clients will be drawn to you.

P-Poka's first lead finally came through, thanks to these efforts. There is a special thrill in securing that first one, as any business owner will attest. Especially because it's the first step on the long road to scaling — from one, to one million.

To learn more or for access to tons of free resources, visit www.marketingscaleur.com or follow me on Twitter and LinkedIn (https://twitter.com/MScaleurs, https://www.linkedin.com/company/38104174). I look forward to helping you scale your marketing and overall business.

Acknowledgments

I would like to thank my mentor, Lionel Benizri, who gave me the energy and push to go the extra mile in setting up Scaleurs, a company focusing on scaling all parts of a business. He convinced me to go from the safety and security of the corporate world to taking a risk and starting my own business.

I would also like to thank Joost Smaal at Unibake. Joost helped start the Shiny Happy People team for the company. When he left Unibake, he gave me a compass with the words "If you can dream it, you can do it." Follow your inner compass, and you will do great things!

And finally, thanks to my friends and family, who have already added the word *scaleur* to their dictionaries and are starting to think daily about objectives to accomplish. They also help me remember not to focus only on work, but that we must *live* — have fun and enjoyment while working!

About the Author

Jolien Demeyer has over 10 years of experience as an export manager, senior category manager, and marketing director for some of the biggest names in the foodservice industry. A voracious learner and consummate autodidact, she holds three master's degrees in business, management, and accounting, and she owns and operates her own marketing consultancy, Marketing Scaleurs. Originally from Belgium, she currently resides in Chicago.

INDEX

f following a page number denotes a figure
n following a page number denotes a footnote

W

wave.video, 80
Web 2 Media (W2M), 101–102
webinars, 81
website content, repurposing/
recycling of, 76–86, 141
website designer/webmaster, as
one of nine positions in winning
marketing team, 34–36
website performance, as part of
marketing strategy plan, 55
website SEO/PPC tools
Google Ads, 132–133
Keyword Too, 132
Optimize, 131–132
Semrush, 132
Unbounce, 131
website traffic, measurement of,
98, 109–110
white papers, 78–79
WordPress (WP) plugins, 79, 106

Y

your life, making work part of
your life, not your life itself,
121–122
YouTube, use of, 76, 86, 89, 134

Z

Zapier, 88, 107, 129
Zoom, 52

Made in the USA
Middletown, DE
21 September 2022